Chipmunks and Little Friends

金花鼠和小朋友

Mildred Shaw & Loretta Huang, Ph.D. 杜英慈

One touch of nature makes the whole world kin.
William Shakespeare

接觸自然 四海一家
威廉莎士比亞

jiē chù zì rán　sì hǎi yī jiā
接触自然 四海一家
wēi lián suō shì bǐ yà
威廉莎士比亚

Copyright©2023 by Loretta Huang, Ph.D.
ISBN No. 978-1-63972-868-8

All rights reserved. No portion of this book may be reproduced, stored in a retrieval system or transmitted in any form or by any means---electric, mechanical, photography, recording, scanning, or other---except for brief quotations in critical reviews, without the prior written permission of the publisher or author.

Dedicated to

G. D. W. JL
Katherine, James, Lucas, Nathan
&
All Children Who Love Animals and Nature

❤️ 💙 💚 💙 🩵 💛 🧡 🤎 ❤️

獻(ㄒㄧㄢˋ)給(ㄍㄟˇ)

G. D. W. JL
Katherine, James, Lucas, Nathan

及(ㄐㄧˊ)

所(ㄙㄨㄛˇ)有(ㄧㄡˇ)喜(ㄒㄧˇ)愛(ㄞˋ)動(ㄉㄨㄥˋ)物(ㄨˋ)和(ㄏㄜˊ)自(ㄗˋ)然(ㄖㄢˊ)的(ㄉㄜ˙)小(ㄒㄧㄠˇ)朋(ㄆㄥˊ)友(ㄧㄡˇ)

❤️ 💙 💚 💙 🩵 💛 🧡 🤎 ❤️

xiàn gěi
献给

G. D. W. JL
Katherine, James, Lucas, Nathan

jí
及

suǒ yǒu xǐ ài dòng wù hé zì rán dì xiǎo péng yǒu
所有喜爱动物和自然的小朋友

Contents

Preface ii
前言
qián yán
前言

Happy Chipmunks 2
快樂的金花鼠
kuài lè di jīn huā shǔ
快乐的金花鼠

Easy Riders 42
舒適的小乘客
shū shì di xiǎo chéng kè
舒适的小乘客

Ladybugs 102
小瓢蟲
xiǎo piáo chóng
小瓢虫

The Life and Times of Baby Robins 144
知更鳥寶寶的一生
zhī gēng niǎo bǎo bǎo di yī shēng
知更鸟宝宝的一生

Puppies, Puppies, Puppies 192
小狗、小狗、小狗
xiǎo gǒu xiǎo gǒu xiǎo gǒu
小狗、小狗、小狗

Rabbit Eggs 234
兔子蛋
tù zǐ dàn
兔子蛋

Spider the Web Site 294
蜘蛛網址
zhī zhū wǎng zhǐ
蜘蛛网址

The Wishing Goldfish 338
許願的小金魚
xǔ yuàn di xiǎo jīn yú
许愿的小金鱼

Preface

The rhyming stories on animals, nature, and environment specifically for children ages 3 to 8 are written in English, traditional Chinese with zhuyin, and simplified Chinese with pinyin. The purpose is to help children of the world to learn ENGLISH, TRADITIONAL CHINESE, and SIMPLIFIED CHINESE. These languages are all international languages designated by the United Nations. The rhymes are also to encourage children to appreciate animals and nature to learn to love and protect the environment in which we live.

The unique features of the book include (1) Creative stories in standard English and Chinese characters for young children, (2) Words of Wisdom, (3) Interesting Information about the Animals, and (4) Workshop Activities that encourage children and adult interactions to develop children's listening, speaking, reading and writing skills as well as children's artistic, creative, observational, research, and social talents. Difficult words in English are in *Italics*, and correct answers are in **bold**.

The authors of the books are experienced language and reading specialists who love children and have been devoted to life-long learning. **Dr. Loretta Huang** is an expert in Teaching English as a Second Language for over six decades. **Mrs. Mildred Shaw** was a retired reading teacher and art consultant. All of the **illustrators** have been teenagers and young adults in their twenties. Their artistic styles are realistic, sketches, and electronic arts.

It is our hope that children who read the book will enjoy learning English and Chinese AND appreciate the beauty and marvel of nature.

前言

　　這些有關動物、自然、環保的押韻故事，是為3至8歲兒童寫的，是英文、繁體中文與注音、和簡體中文與拼音的雙語讀物。目的是幫助兒童學習英文、正體中文、和簡體中文。這些語文都是聯合國公定的世界語文。這本兒童書也是要鼓勵小朋友欣賞動物和自然，學習關愛和保護我們居住的環境。

　　故事書的特色是 (1) 適合兒童年齡的標準中英文創意故事，(2) 小小智慧之語，(3) 有關該動物的有趣知識，(4) 工作室，鼓勵孩子與大人互動，發展兒童聽、說、讀、寫的能力，及發揮兒童藝術創作觀察研究及社交的天分。不熟的英文字是用斜體字，正確的知識是粗體字。

　　這本書的作者都是喜愛兒童和獻身終身學習及富有經驗的語言教學專家。杜英慈博士是60多年的英語教學專家。Mrs. Mildred Shaw 是退休的閱讀和藝術顧問教師。所有的插圖都是青少年畫的，有寫實、描繪、和電子構圖的藝術風格。

　　我們希望讀了這本書的小朋友，都喜歡學習英文和中文，也都欣賞、愛好、讚歎自然之美。

iii

前言

这些有关动物、自然、环保的押韵故事，是为3至8岁儿童写的，是英文、繁体中文与注音、和简体中文与拼音的双语读物。这本儿童书是要鼓励小朋友欣赏动物和自然，学习关爱和保护我们居住的环境。

故事书的特色是（1）适合儿童年龄的标准中英文创意故事，（2）小小智慧之语，（3）有关该动物的有趣知识，（4）工作室，鼓励孩子与大人互动，发展儿童听、说、读、写的能力，以及发挥儿童艺术创作、观察研究、及社交的天分。不熟的英文字是用斜体字，正确的知识是用粗体字。

这本书的作者都是喜爱儿童和献身终身学习及富有经验的语言教学专家。杜英慈博士是60多年的英语教学专家。Mrs. Mildred Shaw 是退休的阅读和艺术顾问教师。所有的插图都是青少年画的，有写实、描绘、和电子艺术的艺术风格。

我们希望读了这本书的小朋友，都喜欢学习英文和中文，也都欣赏、爱好、赞叹自然之美。

"Happy Chipmunks" is the story of two chipmunks getting ready for tourists to visit them. After they enjoy the good food tourist have given them, they find a clever way to store extra food and to clean up the environment.

"快樂的金花鼠"描寫兩隻金花鼠準備好，等待遊客來到。當它們吃完遊客給的美味食物之後，它們想到一個好方法把多餘的食物收藏起來，也把四周的環境整理清潔。

"快乐的金花鼠"描写两只金花鼠准备好，等待游客来到。当它们吃完游客给的美味食物之后，它们想到一个好方法把多余的食物收藏起来，也把四周的环境整理清洁。

"Easy Rider" is a story about two little ants that find a snail to take them around and enjoy true bounding friendship.

"舒適的小乘客"兩隻小螞蟻遇見了一隻蝸牛帶著它們閒逛而變成真正親蜜的好朋友。

"舒适的小乘客"两只小蚂蚁遇见了一只蜗牛带着它们闲逛而变成真正亲密的好朋友。

"Ladybugs" is a story on tiny, lucky insects that help keep our garden free from harmful bugs.

"小瓢蟲"描寫體型微小，會帶來好運的小蟲，幫助我們除去花園裏的害蟲。

"小瓢虫"描写体型微小，会带来好运的小虫，帮助我们除去花园里的害虫。

"The Life and Times of Baby Robins" is the story of three Robin babies who have Mother Robin Red Breast working so hard to feed them and teach them to fly. When the babies grow up, they carefully try their wings and say goodbye to their Mother.

"知更鳥寶寶的一生"是一隻紅胸脯知更鳥媽媽忙碌地喂養三隻知更鳥寶寶，又教它們飛翔。當寶寶們長大了，它們開心地拍著翅膀向媽媽快樂地說再見的故事。

"知更鸟宝宝的一生"是一只红胸脯知更鸟妈妈忙碌地喂养三只知更鸟宝宝，又教它们飞翔。当宝宝们长大了，它们开心地拍着翅膀向妈妈快乐地说再见的故事。

"**Puppies, Puppies, Puppies**" is the story of three puppies that are in a pet store waiting to be taken home to make excellent pets for a family.

"小狗,小狗,小狗"是三隻小狗的故事。它們在寵物店等待一家人把它們帶回家做最好的寵物朋友。

"小狗,小狗,小狗"是三只小狗的故事。它们在宠物店等待一家人把它们带回家做最好的宠物朋友。

"**Rabbit Eggs**" is the story of many rabbits living in Rabbit Town underground, which make colorful and tasty eggs day and night for children and adults. Do you want to know why?

"兔子蛋"的故事是描述住在地底下兔子鎮的兔子日夜忙碌,製作彩色美味的糖蛋給小朋友和大人吃。你想知道為什麼嗎?

"兔子蛋"的故事是描述住在地底下兔子镇的兔子日夜忙碌,制作彩色美味的糖蛋给小朋友和大人吃。你想知道为什么吗?

"Spider the Web Site" A tiny, tiny spider tell us what she loves to do to help humankind.

"蜘蛛網址" 一隻小小的蜘蛛告訴我們她喜歡做的事來幫助人類。

"蜘蛛网址" 一只小小的蜘蛛告诉我们她喜欢做的事来帮助人类。

"The Wishing Gold Fish" Two gold fish got so bored living in a little glass bowl. They were tired of the stale fish food. They wish they could have wings to fly. Suddenly, a mermaid appeared and granted their wish!

"許願的金魚" 兩條金魚住在小玻璃缽裡太無聊了，它們也厭煩吃變味的魚食，它們希望能有翅膀飛翔。忽然，一條美人魚出現滿足了它們的願望！

"许愿的金鱼" 两条金鱼住在小玻璃钵里太无聊了，它们也厌烦吃变味的鱼食，它们希望能有翅膀飞翔。忽然，一条美人鱼出现满足了它们的愿望！

TREASURES

You may have fabulous riches untold
Coffers of silver and coffers of gold.
Wealthier that I, you never will be
Because I have parents who read stories to me.

Anonymous

寶藏

你可能有無數驚人的財富
有大寶庫的金銀財物。
可是你永遠不會比我更富足
因為我有父母親讀故事領我悟。

— 無名氏 —

宝藏

你可能有无数惊人的财富
有大宝库的金银财物。
可是你永远不会比我更富足
因为我有父母亲读故事领我悟。

— 无名氏 —

Happy Chipmunks

快樂的金花鼠

kuài lè dí jīn huā shǔ
快乐的金花鼠

Mildred Shaw & Dr. Loretta Huang 杜英慈 (dù yīng cí)

Illustrated by Gine Chang 张彦珺 (zhāng yàn jùn)

Happy Chipmunks

快樂的金花鼠
kuài lè di jīn huā shǔ
快乐的金花鼠

Two little Chipmunks sitting in the sun,
Happy that winter weather is all done.
They're waiting for some tourists to appear
Tourist are people that they hold so dear.
"What are tourists?" children often ask.
"They're friends that bring chipmunks food that last.
They come here in an enormous car
And stop when they find us where we are."
We have washed our faces so they are clean
And fluffed up our tails so we can be seen.
They know us all by the stripe on our back
That is so shiny and complete black.
Tourists like to throw us peanuts galore;
We eat them until we can eat no more.
We hold that nut in our front paws,
And break that shell with our tiny jaws.
Still on the ground many peanuts lay;
We must think of something without delay.
Really, quickly we've got to make a plan
To save as many peanuts as we can.
One smart chipmunk has gotten very bold
And rolled a pop bottle into its hole.
"We've carried the nuts to the bottle in the ground
Till not a single peanut can be found.
Oh how good those peanuts will later taste!
And not a single one will go to waste!"

Words of wisdom:

Waste not, Want not!

智慧之語：不浪費，不缺乏！惜福得福！
zhì huì zhī yǔ   bù làng fèi   bù quē fá   xī fú dé fú
智慧之语：不浪费，不缺乏！惜福得福！

Happy Chipmunks

Two little Chipmunks sitting in the sun,
Happy that winter weather is all done.

快樂的金花鼠

兩隻小金花鼠坐在太陽下，
好高興冬天的冷氣候已經過去了呀。

kuài lè di jīn huā shǔ
快乐的金花鼠

liǎng zhǐ xiǎo jīn huā shǔ zuò zài tài yáng xià
两只小金花鼠坐在太阳下，
hǎo gāo xìng dōng tiān di lěng qì hòu yǐ jīng guò qù liǎo yā
好高兴冬天的冷气候已经过去了呀。

Happy Chipmunks

They're waiting for some tourists to appear;
Tourist are people that they hold so dear.

它們在等待一些遊客出現；
遊客是它們最親愛喜愛的人。

tā men zài děng dài yī xiē yóu kè chū xiàn
它们在等待一些游客出现；
yóu kè shì tā men zuì qīn ài xǐ ài dì rén
游客是它们最亲爱喜爱的人。

Happy Chipmunks

"What are tourists?" children often ask.
"They're friends that bring chipmunks food that last.

小孩兒常常問,"什麼是遊客?"
"他們是帶給金花鼠很多食物的朋友。

小孩儿常常问,"什么是游客?"
"他们是带给金花鼠很多食物的朋友。

Happy Chipmunks

They come here in an enormous car
And stop when they find us where we are."

他們開一輛大車子到這兒來
當他們找到我們就馬上停下來。"

tā men kāi yī liàng dà chē zǐ dào zhè ér lái
他们开一辆大车子到这儿来
dāng tā men zhǎo dào wǒ men jiù mǎ shàng tíng xià lái
当他们找到我们就马上停下来。"

Happy Chipmunks

We have washed our faces so they are clean
And fluffed up our tails so we can be seen.

我們已經洗好了臉，所以臉很乾淨
也把尾巴抖開，這樣我們能被看見看清。

wǒ men yǐ jīng xǐ hǎo liǎo liǎn　suǒ yǐ liǎn hěn gān jìng
我们已经洗好了脸，所以脸很干净
yě bǎ wěi bā dǒu kāi　zhè yàng wǒ men néng bèi kàn jiàn kàn qīng
也把尾巴抖开，这样我们能被看见看清。

Happy Chipmunks

They know us all by the stripe on our back,
That is so shiny and complete black.

遊客看到我們背上的條紋就認得我們，
條紋是發亮又全黑。

yóu kè kàn dào wǒ men bèi shàng di tiáo wén jiù rèn dé wǒ men
游客看到我们背上的条纹就认得我们，
tiáo wén shì fā liàng yòu quán hēi
条纹是发亮又全黑。

Happy Chipmunks

Tourists like to throw us peanuts galore;
We eat them until we can eat no more.

遊客喜歡丟給我們許多花生；
一直到我們再也吃不下那麼多花生。

yóu kè xǐ huān diū gěi wǒ men xǔ duō huā shēng
游客喜欢丢给我们许多花生；
zhí dào wǒ men zài yě chī bù xià nà me duō huā shēng
直到我们再也吃不下那么多花生。

Happy Chipmunks

We hold that nut in our front paws,
And break that shell with our tiny jaws.

我們把花生拿在我們的兩隻前爪子裏，
然後用我們小小的上下顎咬開硬殼兒。

wǒ men bǎ huā shēng ná zài wǒ men dì liǎng zhǐ qián zhǎo zǐ lǐ
我们把花生拿在我们的两只前爪子里，
rán hòu yòng wǒ men xiǎo xiǎo dì shàng xià è yǎo kāi yìng ké ér
然后用我们小小的上下颚咬开硬壳儿。

Still on the ground many peanuts lay;
We must think of something without delay.

在地上還是有很多花生；
我們必須想個好法子不要拖延。

zài dì shàng huán shì yǒu hěn duō huā shēng
在地上还是有很多花生；
wǒ men bì xū xiǎng gè hǎo fǎ zǐ bù yào tuō yán
我们必须想个好法子不要拖延。

Really, quickly we've got to make a plan
To save as many peanuts as we can.

真的，我們必須儘快做個好計劃
儘我們能力把這些花生都存起來吧。

zhēn dì　　wǒ men bì xū jìn kuài zuò gè hǎo jì huà
真的，我们必须尽快做个好计划
jìn wǒ men néng lì bǎ zhè xiē huā shēng dū cún qǐ lái bā
尽我们能力把这些花生都存起来吧。

Happy Chipmunks

One smart chipmunk has gotten very bold
And rolled a pop bottle into its hole.

一隻ㄓ聰ㄘㄨㄥ明ㄇㄧㄥ的ㄉㄜ金ㄐㄧㄣ花ㄏㄨㄚ鼠ㄕㄨ變ㄅㄧㄢ成ㄔㄥ非ㄈㄟ常ㄔㄤ勇ㄩㄥ敢ㄍㄢˇ
就ㄐㄧㄡ滾ㄍㄨㄣ動ㄉㄨㄥ一一個ㄍㄜ汽ㄑㄧ水ㄕㄨㄟ瓶ㄆㄧㄥ進ㄐㄧㄣ到ㄉㄠ它ㄊㄚ的ㄉㄜ洞ㄉㄨㄥ穴ㄒㄩㄝ裏ㄌㄧ。

yī zhǐ cōng míng dì jīn huā shǔ biàn chéng fēi cháng yǒng gǎn
一只聪明的金花鼠变成非常勇敢
jiù gǔn dòng liǎo yī gè qì shuǐ píng jìn dào tā dì dòng xué lǐ
就滚动了一个气水瓶进到它的洞穴里。

"We've carried the nuts to the bottle
in the ground
Till not a single peanut can be found.

我們把花生搬運到地下的汽水瓶裏
一直到花生在地上也找不到一粒。

wǒ men bǎ huā shēng bān yùn dào dì xià dì qì shuǐ píng lǐ
我们把花生搬运到地下的气水瓶里
yī zhí dào huā shēng zài dì shàng yě zhǎo bù dào yī lì
一直到花生在地上也找不到一粒。

Oh how good those peanuts will later taste!
And not a single one will go to waste!"

啊！這些花生以後吃起來多麼美味！
而且一粒花生也沒浪費！

啊！这些花生以后吃起来多么美味！
而且一粒花生也没浪费！

Interesting Facts about Chipmunks for Children

1. Chipmunk is a small, *striped*, ground-living animal in Asia and North America that lives in *burrows* (*tunnels*).
2. The eastern chipmunk is larger than most of the western chipmunks.
3. American chipmunk has light-colored *stripes* on the face, back, and sides. Black *borders* the *stripes*. The rest of the back, legs, and tail are reddish-brown. The underside of a chipmunk is light gray or white.
4. Most American chipmunks are about 8 inches (20 *centimeters*) long *including* the tail, and weigh about 1.8 ounces (51 grams).
5. Chipmunks are rodents, in the same family as *squirrels*.
6. Chipmunks hop along on strong hind legs, *searching* for food.
7. Chipmunks' diets also include birds' egg, worms, snails, insects, *fungi*, berries, seeds, nuts, grains, fruits, grass, leaves, and vegetables.
8. They eat by holding a piece of food in their small, slender front paws and *nibbling* at it with their sharp front teeth.
9. Chipmunks store food in their *tunnels* (*burrows*). They can store up to eight pounds of food.
10. Chipmunks store shells and *droppings* in *refuse tunnels*.
11. *Burrows* can be up to 30 feet (9.1 meters) in length and have several *entrances*.
12. Their sleeping *quarters* in the burrows are kept *extremely* clean.
13. Chipmunks sleep (*hibernate*) from late fall through winter to early spring, but they may awaken on warm winter days and eat some of their food.
14. Most *female* chipmunks bear from two to eight young (a) once a year (b) **twice a year** (c) three times a year.
15. Young chipmunks are grown by three months.
16. If not becoming *victims* of hawks and meat-eating animals, chipmunks may live (a) **2 to 3 years** (b) 4 to 5 years (c) 6 to 7 years.
17. It is **NOT** safe to pick up and pet wild chipmunks.

給小朋友
關于金花鼠的有趣知識

1. 金花鼠是亞洲及北美洲住在地洞隧道裏有條紋的動物。
2. 東方的金花鼠比多數西方的金花鼠大些。
3. 美洲的金花鼠在臉上、背上和旁邊有淡色的條紋。條紋有黑邊。背上其他部分，腳和尾巴都是紅棕色。金花鼠肚子底下是灰色或白色。
4. 大多數的美洲金花鼠連尾巴有8英吋長（約21厘米），大約重1.8盎司（51公克）。
5. 金花鼠是嚙齒動物像兔子和松鼠一樣。
6. 金花鼠用強壯的後腿跳躍尋找食物。
7. 金花鼠的食物包括鳥蛋、軟虫、蝸牛、昆虫、菌類、漿果、种子、硬果、穀粒、水果、小草、葉子、和蔬菜等。
8. 它們用細小的前腳握住食物，用尖銳的前齒小口咬著吃。
9. 金花鼠把食物儲存在地下隧道裏。它們能儲存幾乎8磅的食物。
10. 金花鼠把不能吃的硬殼和排泄物存放在垃圾地洞裏。
11. 金花鼠的地洞隧道可以到30英尺長（約9.1米）。
12. 它們地洞隧道裏睡覺的地方非常乾淨整潔。
13. 金花鼠冬眠，從深秋、冬天、到初春它們睡覺。但是冬天暖和的日子，它們會醒來吃些食物。
14. 母金花鼠一次生2-8只寶寶。（a）一年一次 （b）一年兩次 （c）一年三次。
15. 年輕的金花鼠三個月就長大了。
16. 假如不被老鷹或肉食動物吃掉，金花鼠能活 （a）兩、三年 （b）四、五年 （c）六、七年。
17. 把野生金花鼠拿起拍摸是不安全的。

给小朋友
关于金花鼠的有趣知识

1. 金花鼠是亚洲及北美洲住在地洞隧道里有条纹的动物。
2. 东方的金花鼠比多数西方的金花鼠大些。
3. 美洲的金花鼠在脸上、背上和旁边有淡色的条纹。条纹有黑边。背上其他部分，脚和尾巴都是红棕色。金花鼠肚子底下是灰色或白色。
4. 大多数的美洲金花鼠连尾巴有8英寸长（约21厘米），大约重1.8盎司(51公克)。
5. 金花鼠是啮齿动物像兔子和松鼠一样。
6. 金花鼠用强壮的後腿跳跃寻找食物。
7. 金花鼠的食物包括鸟蛋、软虫、蜗牛、昆虫、菌类、浆果、种子、硬果、谷粒、水果、小草、叶子、和蔬菜等。
8. 它们用细小的前脚握住食物，用尖锐的前齿小口咬着吃。
9. 金花鼠把食物储存在地下隧道里。它们能储存几乎8磅的食物。
10. 金花鼠把不能吃的硬壳和排泄物存放在垃圾地洞里。
11. 金花鼠的地洞隧道可以到30英尺长（约9.1米）。
12. 它们地洞隧道里睡觉的地方非常乾净整洁。
13. 金花鼠冬眠，从深秋、冬天、到初春它们睡觉。但是冬天暖和的日子，它们醒来吃些食物。
14. 母金花鼠一次生2-8只宝宝。(a)一年一次 （b）**一年两次**（c）一年三次。
15. 年轻的金花鼠三个月就长大了。
16. 假如不被老鹰或肉食动物吃掉，金花鼠能活（a）**两、三年**（b）四、五年（c）六、七年。
17. 把野生金花鼠拿起拍摸是不安全的。

Chipmunk Workshop for Children

1. Look at the pictures of chipmunks and describe them to your parents, grandparents, or teachers.

2. Tell your parents, grandparents, or teachers what you would do when you see wild chipmunks.

3. Would you like to color the picture of the chipmunk or draw a picture of a chipmunk or more chipmunks?

4. Find books in the library or surf the web for information about chipmunks. Read the material and tell your parents, grandparents, or teachers about chipmunks.

5. How do we protect the natural environment when we visit parks? Tell your parents, grandparents, or teachers your bright ideas on environmental protection.

小朋友的金花鼠工作室

1. 仔細看看這些金花鼠的圖片。描述給你的爸爸媽媽、祖父母或老師聽,你看到什麼?

2. 告訴你的爸爸媽媽、祖父母或老師,當你看到野生金花鼠的時候,你要做什麼?

3. 你要不要把工作室的金花鼠塗上顏色或是畫一隻或幾隻金花鼠?

4. 在圖書館或網上找一些金花鼠的資訊。讀了以後告訴你的爸爸媽媽、祖父母或老師你學到有關金花鼠的寶貴知識。

5. 我們去公園的時候,大家如何保護自然環境呢?告訴你的爸爸、媽媽、祖父母或老師,你保護自然環境的好主意。

小朋友的金花鼠工作室

1. 仔细看看这些金花鼠的图片。描述给你的爸爸妈妈、祖父母或老师听,你看到什么?

2. 告诉你的爸爸妈妈、祖父母或老师,当你看到野生金花鼠的时候,你要做什么?

3. 你要不要工作室的金花鼠涂上颜色或画一只或几只金花鼠?

4. 在图书馆或网上找一些金花鼠的资讯。读了以后告诉你的爸爸妈妈、祖父母或老师你学到有关金花鼠的宝贵知识。

5. 我们去公园的时候,我们大家如何保护自然环境呢?告诉你的爸爸、妈妈、祖父母或老师,你保护自然环境的好主意。

金ㄐㄧㄣ 花ㄏㄨㄚ 鼠ㄕㄨ Chipmunk 金花鼠
Jīn Huā Shǔ

Easy Riders

舒ㄕㄨ適ㄕˋ的ㄉㄜ˙ 小ㄒㄧㄠˇ乘ㄔㄥˊ客ㄎㄜˋ

shū shì dì xiǎo chéng kè
舒适的小乘客

Mildred Shaw & Dr. Loretta Huang 杜ㄉㄨˋ英ㄧㄥ慈ㄘˊ

Illustrated by Grace Novelly

Easy Riders

舒適的小乘客
shū shì dì xiǎo chéng kè
舒适的小乘客

Two little ants were crawling on the ground.
One ant said, "We're slow, I've found!"
Perhaps that smooth grass
would provide us ease,
So we could move forward
as fast as we please.
We are down so low that we cannot see
Any flower, or bird, or cloud, or tree.
Nobody else wants an ant for a friend;
Our life is dull from beginning to end.
We cannot buzz or seldom sting or bite;
Nor run very fast, or fly out of sight.
We are only insects without a friend;
Were stepped on, sprayed on,
until our lives end.

The two little ants were so tired, they said,
When they saw a slow moving bump ahead.
"It's Mr. Snail gliding slowly away.
Maybe he will give us a ride today."
Could we hitch a ride on top of your shell?"
"Sure," said the snail."You can ride there quite well?'
"Why snails have no friends, we ants don't ever know.
You're a friend to us and keep us on the go."
"To us ants, you're like a large limousine,
When we're with you, were happy to be seen."

They went along until Mr. Snail said,
"I'm hungry and know when we can be fed.
Peaches from trees have fallen on the ground.
And they are the best meal I've ever found."
"Good night," said Mr. Snail, "I wish you well.
If you want you can sleep under my shell."
The two ants agreed that sounded so good,
And everything went as well as it could.
The three friends gaily bonded together,
And stayed so close, no matter the weather.

Words of wisdom:

A friend in need is a friend indeed.

智慧之語：在你需要的時候，幫助你的朋友才是真正的朋友。

zhì huì zhī yǔ　　zài nǐ xū yào dí shí hòu　　bāng zhù nǐ dí péng yǒu cái shì zhēn zhèng dí péng yǒu

智慧之语：在你需要的时候，帮助你的朋友才是真正的朋友。

Easy Riders

Two little ants were crawling on the ground.
One ant said, "We're slow, I've found!"

舒ㄕㄨ適ㄕˋ的˙小ㄒㄧㄠˇ乘ㄔㄥˊ客ㄎㄜˋ

兩ㄌㄧㄤˇ隻ㄓ小ㄒㄧㄠˇ螞ㄇㄚˇ蟻ㄧˇ沿ㄧㄢˊ著˙地ㄉㄧˋ上ㄕㄤˋ爬ㄆㄚˊ。

一ㄧ隻ㄓ對ㄉㄨㄟˋ另ㄌㄧㄥˋ一ㄧ隻ㄓ說ㄕㄨㄛ, " 我ㄨㄛˇ認ㄖㄣˋ為ㄨㄟˊ我ㄨㄛˇ們˙

走ㄗㄡˇ得˙好ㄏㄠˇ慢ㄇㄢˋ呀˙！"

shū shì dì xiǎo chéng kè
舒 适 的 小 乘 客

liǎng zhī xiǎo mǎ yǐ yán zhù dì shàng pá
两 只 小 蚂 蚁 沿 著 地 上 爬。

yī zhī duì lìng yī zhī shuō　　　　wǒ rèn wéi wǒ men zǒu dé hǎo màn yā
一 只 对 另 一 只 说, "我 认 为 我 们 走 得 好 慢 呀！"

Perhaps that smooth grass
would provide us ease,
So we could move forward
as fast as we please.

假如我們走在平滑的青草地會更容易，
我們向前走的速度會更如意。

jiǎ rú wǒ men zǒu zài píng huá dì qīng cǎo dì huì gēng róng yì
假如我们走在平滑的青草地会更容易，
wǒ men xiàng qián zǒu dì sù dù huì gēng rú yì
我们向前走的速度会更如意。

Easy Riders

We are down so low that we cannot see
Any flower, or bird, or cloud, or tree.

我們低矮地爬在地上什麼也看不到
像花朵、　鳥兒、　雲彩、　和樹梢。

wǒ men dī ǎi dì pá zài dì shàng shí me yě kàn bù dào
我们低矮地爬在地上什么也看不到
xiàng huā duǒ　niǎo ér　yún cǎi　hé shù shāo
像花朵、鸟儿、云彩、和树梢。

Nobody else wants an ant for a friend;
Our life is dull from beginning to end.

沒ㄇㄟˊ人ㄖㄣˊ要ㄧㄠˋ跟ㄍㄣ一ㄧ隻ㄓ螞ㄇㄚˇ蟻ㄧˇ做ㄗㄨㄛˋ朋ㄆㄥˊ友ㄧㄡˇ；
我ㄨㄛˇ們ㄇㄣ的ㄉㄜ˙生ㄕㄥ活ㄏㄨㄛˊ從ㄘㄨㄥˊ頭ㄊㄡˊ到ㄉㄠˋ尾ㄨㄟˇ都ㄉㄡ是ㄕˋ枯ㄎㄨ燥ㄗㄠˋ無ㄨˊ聊ㄌㄧㄠˊ。

méi rén yào gēn yī zhǐ mǎ yǐ zuò péng yǒu
没人要跟一只蚂蚁做朋友
wǒ men dì shēng huó cóng tóu dào wěi dū shì kū zào wú liáo
我们的生活从头到尾都是枯燥无聊。

Easy Riders

We cannot buzz, or seldom sting or bite;
Nor run very fast, or fly out of sight.

我們不會叫， 很少叮也很少咬；
不會快快跑， 也不會飛得高。

wǒ men bù huì jiào　　hěn shǎo dīng yě hěn shǎo yǎo
我们不会叫，很少叮也很少咬；
　bù huì kuài kuài pǎo　　yě bù huì fēi dé gāo
不会快快跑，也不会飞得高。

Easy Riders

We are only insects without a friend;
We're stepped on, sprayed on,
until our lives end.

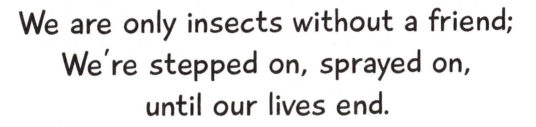

我们只是没有朋友的昆虫；
我们被踩到或被杀虫剂喷到，就死掉。

Easy Riders

The two little ants were so tired, they said,
When they saw a slow moving bump ahead.

小㆗媽㆐蟻㆒說㆙它㆝們㆑走㆗得㆓好㆒疲㆐倦㆛,
正㆗好㆕它㆝們㆑看㆔到㆕一一塊㆖慢㆑慢㆑在㆕移㆒動㆑的㆑
東㆛西㆓在㆕前㆑面㆑。

两只小蚂蚁说它们走得好疲倦,
正好它们看到一块慢慢地在移动的
东西在前面。

"It's Mr. Snail gliding slowly away.
Maybe he will give us a ride today."

"那是蝸牛先生慢慢地滑動。
說不定他今天會給我們搭個便車。"

"那是蜗牛先生慢慢地滑动。
说不定他今天会给我们搭个便车。"

Easy Riders

Could we hitch a ride on top of your shell?"
"Sure," said the snail.
"You can ride there quite well."

"我們能不能在你的背殼上搭一個便車?"
"當然可以!" 蝸牛說, "你們
可以好好地坐在上面。"

"我们能不能在你的背壳上搭一个便车?"
"当然可以!" 蜗牛说, "你们
可以好好地坐在上面。"

"Why snails have no friends,
we ants don't ever know.
You're a friend to us and keep us on the go."

" 為什麼蝸牛沒有朋友， 我們螞蟻也不知道。
你是我們的朋友， 幫助我們往前走。 "

"为什么蜗牛没有朋友，我们蚂蚁也不知道。
你是我们的朋友，帮助我们往前走。"

"To us ants, you're like a large limousine,
When we're with you,
we're happy to be seen."

"對我們螞蟻來說，你像是一輛
大型的豪華轎車，
當我們和你在一起，我們很開心
被人看到坐大轎車。"

duì wǒ men mǎ yǐ lái shuō nǐ xiàng shì yī liàng
"对我们蚂蚁来说，你像是一辆
dà xíng dì háo huá jiào chē
大型的豪华轿车，
dāng wǒ men hé nǐ zài yī qǐ wǒ men hěn kāi xīn
当我们和你在一起，我们很开心
bèi rén kàn dào zuò dà jiào chē
被人看到坐大轿车。"

Easy Riders

They went along until Mr. Snail said,
"I'm hungry and know where we can be fed.

他們走了好一會兒， 蝸牛先生就說，
"我餓了，我知道我們可以去那兒吃飯。

tā men zǒu liǎo hǎo yī huì ér　　wō niú xiān shēng jiù shuō
他们走了好一会儿，蜗牛先生就说，
wǒ è liǎo　　wǒ zhī dào wǒ men kě yǐ qù nà ér chī fàn
"我饿了，我知道我们可以去那儿吃饭。

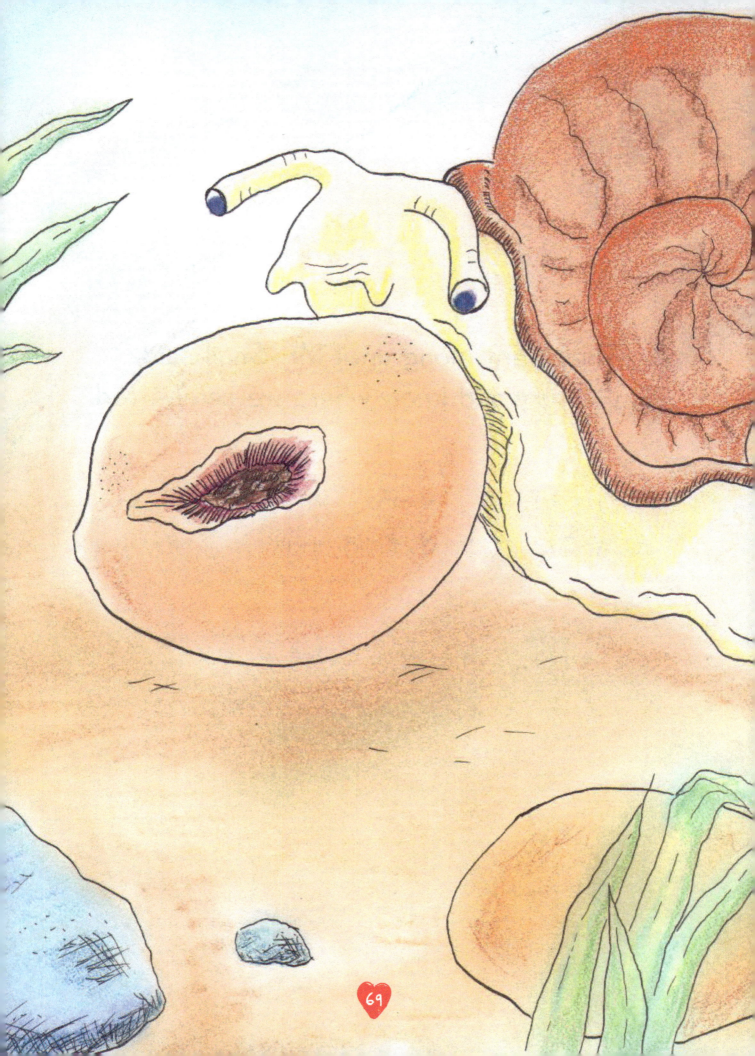

Peaches from trees have fallen on the ground.
And they are the best meal I've ever found."

很多桃子從樹上掉在地上。
那是我找到的最美味的晚餐。"

hěn duō táo zǐ cóng shù shàng diào zài dì shàng
很多桃子从树上掉在地上。
nà shì wǒ zhǎo dào dì zuì měi wèi dì wǎn cān
那是我找到的最美味的晚餐。"

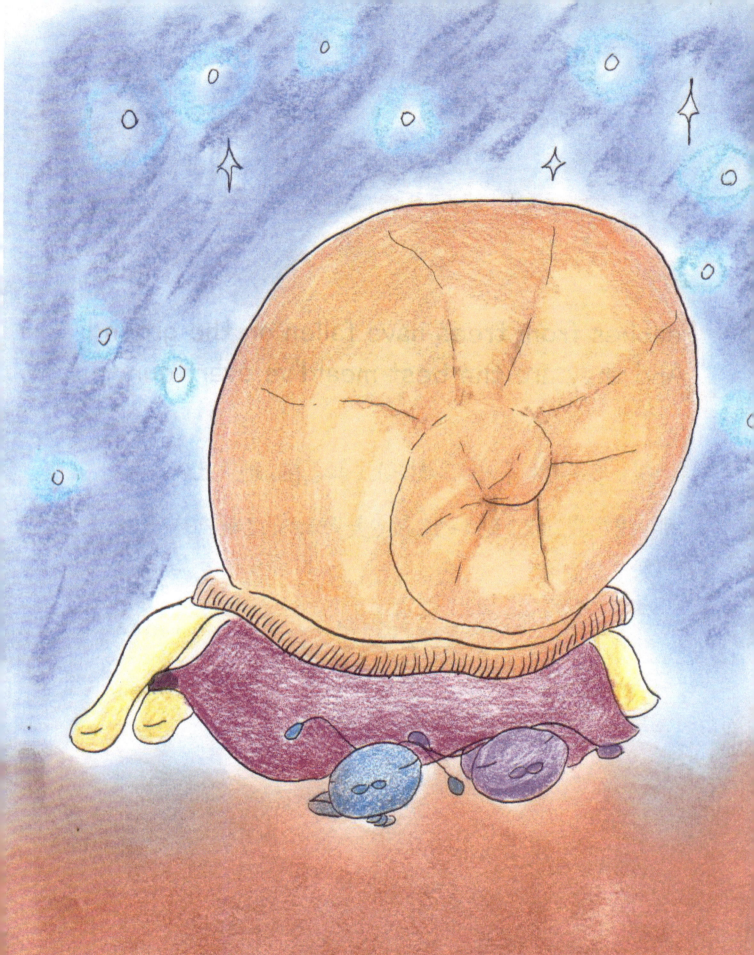

Easy Riders

"Good night," said Mr. Snail, "I wish you well. If you want you can sleep under my shell?"

吃完了，蝸牛先生說，"晚安，
我祝你們健康。
如果你們想睡，在我的背殼底下
你們可以和我一塊兒同享。"

chī wán liǎo   wō niú xiān shēng shuō   wǎn ān
吃完了，蝸牛先生 说，"晚安，
　　　　　　　　wǒ zhù nǐ men jiàn kāng
　　　　　　　　我祝你们健康。
rú guǒ nǐ men xiǎng shuì   zài wǒ dì bèi ké dǐ xià
如果你们想睡，在我的背壳底下
nǐ men kě yǐ hé wǒ yī kuài ér tóng xiǎng
你们可以和我一块儿同享。"

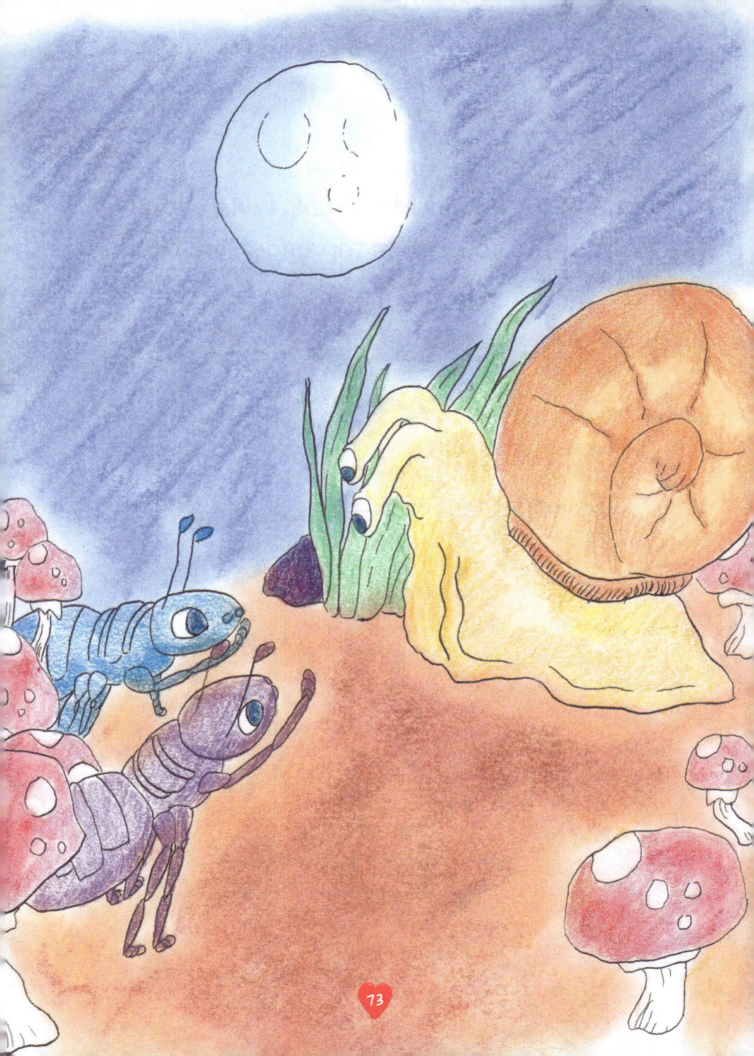

The two ants agreed that sounded so good,
And everything went as well as it could.

两隻小螞蟻同意那是真好的主意，
每一件事都是那麼如意。

liǎng zhī xiǎo mǎ yǐ tóng yì nà shì zhēn hǎo dì zhǔ yì
两只小蚂蚁同意那是真好的主意，
měi yī jiàn shì dū shì nà me rú yì
每一件事都是那么如意。

The three friends gaily bonded together,
And stayed so close, no matter the weather.

三個朋友很快樂分不開地在一起，
不論天氣如何， 它們都很親近地
生活在一起。

sān gè péng yǒu hěn kuài lè fēn bù kāi dì zài yī qǐ
三个朋友很快乐分不开地在一起，
bù lùn tiān qì rú hé　　tā men dū hěn qīn jìn dì shēng huó zài yī qǐ
不论天气如何，它们都很亲近地生活在一起。

Interesting Information about Ants & Snails for Children

Ants

1. Ants are known as *social* insects because they live in *organized communities* called *colonies*.

2. There are about 22,000 kinds (*species*) of ants. Most kinds have dull colors such as black, brown, or rust, but some are yellow, green, blue, or purple.

3. Ants build many types of *colonies*. Most species build their homes *underground*, carving *chambers* and *tunnels* in the soil.

4. An ant *colony* may have dozens, hundreds, thousands, or *millions* of *members*. Each *colony* has one or several *queens*.

5. A *queen's* chief job is to lay eggs, thousands, all her life. They are several times larger than workers are. Queens live about 10-30 years.

6. Most *members* of a colony are *workers* that like the queen, are *females*. The workers build the colony, search for food, care for the young, and fight *enemies*. The largest workers, which are called *soldiers*, may have a bigger head than the other workers have. Workers may live less than 1 year to more than 5 years.

7. *Males (also called drones)* do not do any work in the *colony*. Their only job is to *mate* with young queens. They live only a few weeks or months before they go on the *mating flight*. After *mating*, the males soon die. They are also larger than workers are.

8. The different kinds of ants vary in size, but most are very small. The smallest kinds are a *fraction* of an inch long; the largest kinds are more than an inch (2.5 *centimeters*) long.

9. Ants are *amazingly* strong. Most ants can lift *objects* 10 times heavier that their bodies. Some can even lift 50 times heavier than their bodies.

10. Ants have very interesting bodies. An ant's head includes two *antennae* covered with fine hairs and spines, a pair of *many-lensed compound* eyes, and a pair of *multi-functional* jaws.

79

11. Ants use their *antennae* to smell one another. In this way, ants *recognize* nest-mates. The *antennae* are *organs* of touch, taste, hearing, and smell.

12. An ant has a small food *pouch* under the mouth opening. Ant nest-mates share food by *regurgitation*. Two ants stand mouth to mouth and one spits up some food for the other. Food is shared by all *members* of a *colony*.

13. An ant has three pairs (6) legs attached to the bottom of the *trunk*. Each leg has nine *segments connected by movable joints*.

14. On each front leg, an ant has two combs, like the combs in the jaw, to clean the other pairs of legs and the *antennae*.

15. Among most species of ants, the males and young queens have two pairs of wings *attached* to the *trunk*. They use their wings only once, at *mating* time. The workers have no wings.

16. Ants go through four stages of growth: (1) egg, (2) *larva*, (3) *pupa*, and (4) *adult*.

17. Spiders, frogs, toads, lizards, birds, and many kinds of insects *prey* on ants. Ants protect themselves against *enemies* by stinging or biting. About half of all ant species have stings; some can spray *poison*.

18. Worker ants from different *colonies* often fight one another when they meet. Some ants have *fierce* battles that *result* in death. The winners may *invade* the rest of the *defeated colony* and carry off the *brood*, which they eat.

19. Ants *communicate* with one another by giving off *chemicals*. These *chemicals* are *produced* by *glands* that open at certain places in the head, *trunk*, or end part of the body. They have *distinctive* smells to which ants are *sensitive*. Various kinds of *chemicals communicate* different *information* such as food *discoveries* and danger alarms.

20. Ants *distinguish* members of their colony from enemies by *odor*. When two ants meet, they smell each other with their *antennae*. If they are nest-mates, the two ants may stand mouth to mouth: one ant then *regurgitates* a drop of *liquid* for the other.

21. Ants play an important role in the *balance* of nature. They catch large numbers of insects and so help keep them from becoming too *plentiful*. They are also an important food source for birds, frogs, lizards, and many other animals.

22. Ants are both *beneficial* and *harmful* to farmers. Some species aid farmers by killing insects that *damage* crops. Ants that dig *underground* nests improve the soil by breaking it up, *loosening* it, and mixing it.

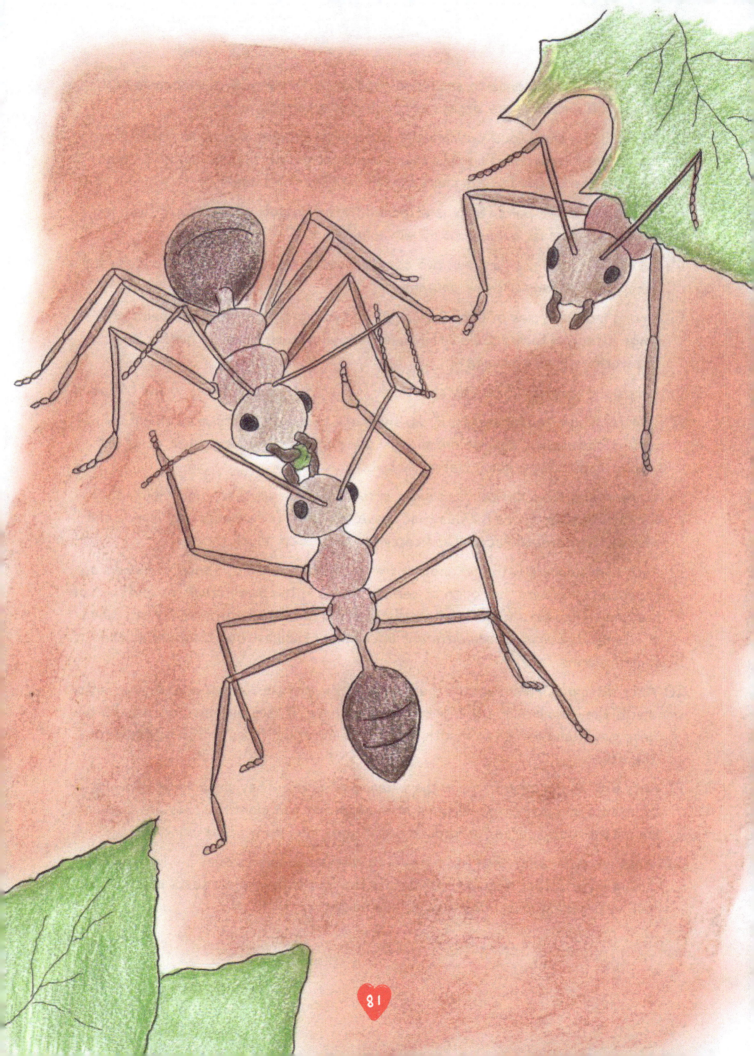

23. Ants can also be pests to farmers by *protecting* pest insects that harm crops; they also have painful stings that cause *allergies* in *humans*.
24. Many kinds of ants are *household* pests that *tunnel* through wooden beams or *invade* houses, restaurants, hospitals, barns, and eat stored food.
25. Before using indoor sprays to *eliminate* ants, make sure that it is *effective* and safe. Using lemon juice and white vinegar on ant trails is safe.
26. Many human *cultures* use ants in *cuisines* and *medicine*.
27. There are no ants in *Antarctica*, a few large islands such as Greenland, Iceland, parts of Polynesia and Hawaii Islands.
28. *Fossils* of ants *indicate* that ants have lived on the earth for more than 100 *million* years.
29. The oldest *amber fossil* of 9.500 *million* years *discovered* in Africa *contains* 28 insects one of which looks like an ant.

Snails

  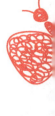

1. A snail is an animal whose *soft body* is usually *covered* with a shell.
2. Its body has a head with feelers (or *tentacles*), eyes, a mouth, and tiny teeth.
3. A snail *creeps* along on a strong *muscular organ* called a foot.
4. A moving snail pours sticky *liquid* called *mucus*, which serves as a pass. During dry weather, the snail seals itself inside its shell with a "door" of dried *mucus*, resting in this *motionless condition* until the dry *spell* ends.
5. There are more than 80,000 kinds of snails---some as small as a *pinhead*, others as long as 2 feet (61 *centimeters*).
6. Snails live almost everywhere: on land, in fresh water (rivers, ponds, lakes, and hot springs), and in the ocean.
7. Snails that live on land have both male and *female sex organs* in the same animals. Most land snails have *lungs*.
8. Most of those that live in water are either *male* or *female*.
9. Some fresh-water snails have *lungs* and must come to the *surface* to breathe the *oxygen* in the air; others have *gills* and can take in *oxygen* from the water.
10. The salt-water (*marine*) snails are the largest group of snails---more than 55,000 kinds living along the seashore or on the ocean floor in the deep part of the ocean. Most of them have *gills*.
11. Land snails *destroy* flowers, vegetables, and plants, but many snails are important food for birds.
12. Some kinds of snails of the Indian and southwest Pacific oceans have a *poisonous stinger* to kill small fish and to cause death to some human beings.
13. Some fresh-water and sea snails that people eat can carry *diseases* if they are taken from *polluted* water.
14. The shells of *turban snails of Australia* are used to make pearly shirt buttons.
15. Many people, especially the French, *consider* a garden snail, known as escargot a great *delicacy*.
16. Snails may live from 2-20 years.

Please surf online for marine snails.

请^{ㄑㄧㄥˇ}上^{ㄕㄤˋ}網^{ㄨㄤˇ}查^{ㄔㄚˊ}詢^{ㄒㄩㄣˊ}"海^{ㄏㄞˇ}螺^{ㄌㄨㄛˊ}。"

qǐng shàng wǎng chá xún hǎi luó
请上网查询"海螺。"

給小朋友
有關螞蟻和蝸牛的有趣常識

螞蟻

1. 螞蟻是群居的昆蟲，因為它們住在有組織的社區，叫做群居螞蟻窩。

2. 螞蟻有兩萬二千種。多數都是暗色，像黑色、棕色、褐色，有的是黃色、綠色、藍色、或紫色。

3. 螞蟻建造很多不同樣子的螞蟻窩。有些種類把窩建在地下，在泥土裏挖穴道和房間。

4. 一個螞蟻窩可能有幾打、幾百，幾千或幾百萬隻螞蟻。每一個群居窩裏有一隻或好幾隻螞蟻皇后。

5. 螞蟻皇后的主要工作就是生蛋，她一生可以生幾千個蛋。她們比工蟻大好幾倍。螞蟻皇后可以活10-30年。

6. 螞蟻窩裏多數的螞蟻是工蟻，像螞蟻皇后一樣，都是母的（雌蟻）。工蟻建造螞蟻窩、尋找食物、照顧寶寶、和敵人打仗。體型最大的工蟻叫做兵蟻，它們的頭比一般工蟻大。工蟻能活一年以下到五年以上。

7. 公的螞蟻（雄蟻）在螞蟻窩裏不做任何事。它們唯一的工作是和年輕的螞蟻皇后交配。在它們做交配飛行之前只活幾個星期或幾個月。交配之後，它們不久就死了。它們也比工蟻大。

8. 不同種類的螞蟻有不同的尺寸，但是大部分體型都很小。最小的螞蟻只有1/25英吋（0.1公分）長。最大的螞蟻有一吋多（2.5公分）長。

9. 螞蟻非常強壯。多數的螞蟻可以抬動比它身體重

10 倍的東西。 有些螞蟻可以抬動重 50 倍的東西。

10. 螞蟻有很有趣的身體。 一只螞蟻頭有兩根長滿細毛和小刺的觸角、 一對（兩個） 多鏡頭的複眼、 和一對（兩個） 多功能的顎。

11. 螞蟻用它們的觸角嗅聞其他的螞蟻。 這樣它們能認得同窩的螞蟻。 觸角是螞蟻觸覺、 味覺、 聽覺、 和嗅覺的器官。

12. 螞蟻在它張開嘴巴的下面有一個小的食物袋。 同窩的螞蟻把食物吐出來分享食物。 兩隻螞蟻嘴對嘴站著， 一隻把食物吐一些給另外的一隻吃。 全螞蟻窩的螞蟻都分享食物。

13. 一隻螞蟻有三對（六隻） 腳長在身體的下面。 每一隻腳有 9 節， 由可以彎的關節連著。

14. 螞蟻每一隻前腳有兩個梳子， 像頭上的梳子一樣， 來清潔其他的腳和觸角。

15. 大多種類的螞蟻， 公蟻（雄蟻） 和小皇后有兩對翅膀長在身體上。 它們只在交配時用一次翅膀。 工蟻沒有翅膀。

16. 螞蟻的成長有四個階段： (1) 卵， (2) 幼蟲， (3) 蛹， (4) 成蟲。

17. 蜘蛛、 青蛙、 蛤蟆、 四腳蛇、 鳥、 和很多種的昆蟲都吃螞蟻。 螞蟻用叮、 咬來抵抗敵人保護自己。 過半數的螞蟻有叮刺， 有些還能噴毒液。

18. 不同螞蟻窩的工蟻在見面時， 會常常打仗。 有些螞蟻打仗激烈造成死亡。 得勝者會侵犯打敗者的螞蟻窩， 把幼蟻帶走當食物。

19. 螞蟻用散發的化學分泌物和別的螞蟻溝通。 這些化學分泌物是從頭部、 身體、 尾部的腺體分泌。 這些化學分泌物有螞蟻敏感的特殊氣味。 不同種的化學分泌物表達不同的資訊，有如"發現食物"和"危險訊號"。

20. 螞蟻用氣味分辨同窩螞蟻或敵人。當兩只螞蟻碰面時，它們用觸角嗅聞對方。如果它們是同窩的，兩隻螞蟻就站著嘴對嘴，一隻螞蟻就把一滴食物吐到另一隻螞蟻的嘴裏。

21. 螞蟻在自然生態平衡上扮演重要的角色。它們吃大量的昆蟲，不讓昆蟲繁殖得太多。螞蟻也是鳥兒、青蛙、四腳蛇和許多動物的食物。

22. 螞蟻對農人有益也有害。有些螞蟻吃損害農作物的害蟲，幫助農人。有些螞蟻在地下挖掘螞蟻窩，把泥土散開、挖鬆、混合，對農人有益。

23. 有些螞蟻保護傷害農作物的害蟲，對農人有害。他們也會叮人咬人，引起人類敏感。

24. 很多種類的螞蟻是家裏的害蟲，它們咬穿木樑侵犯房屋、飯店、醫院、谷倉、還吃存放的食物。

25. 在用噴霧殺蟲劑驅除螞蟻之前，一定要確認那殺蟲劑是安全有效。用檸檬汁和白醋抹在螞蟻走道上是安全的。

26. 很多文化用螞蟻做菜或醫病。

27. 在南極、格林蘭島，冰島、波蘭尼西亞和夏威夷一部分的島沒有土生的螞蟻。

28. 螞蟻化石說明螞蟻在地球上已經有一億年（100,000,000）了。

29. 在非洲發現9500萬年前最古老的琥珀化石中有28種昆蟲，其中一隻像螞蟻。

蝸牛（螺）

1. 蝸牛是一種動物，它的軟身體有一個殼蓋住。

2. 它的身體有一個有觸角的頭、眼睛、一張嘴、和小牙齒。

3. 蝸牛用叫做腳的強壯肌肉爬行。

4. 一隻在爬行的蝸牛大量分泌粘液造成一條狹路好滑行。天氣乾燥的時候，蝸牛用乾的粘液，造成一個門，把自己關在自己的殼子裏面，在不動的情況下休息，等待乾季結束。

5. 世界上已經有8萬（80,000）種蝸牛——有些像針頭一樣小，有些有兩尺（61公分）長。

6. 什麼地方都有蝸牛：在陸地上、在淡水中（河、池、湖、溫泉）、和海洋裏。

7. 住在陸地上的蝸牛是雌雄同體（在身體裏有雌性和雄性器官）。大部分的陸地蝸牛有肺。

8. 大部分住在水裏的蝸牛，不是雌的，就是雄的。（不是雌雄同體。）

9. 有些淡水蝸牛有肺，必需浮到水面來呼吸空氣中的氧氣。有些淡水蝸牛有鰓，可以吸取水中的氧氣。

10. 鹹水（海洋）裏的蝸牛（海螺）是最多的蝸牛——有5萬5千種住在海岸邊或是深海的海底。大部分有鰓。

11. 陸地上的蝸牛損壞花朵、蔬菜、和植物。但是很多蝸牛是鳥兒的好食物。

12. 有些印度洋和太平洋西南方的蝸牛（海螺）有毒刺，可以殺死小魚，也造成人類的死亡。

13. 有些從汙染的淡水和海洋裏的蝸牛（螺）帶病菌，人不能吃。
14. 澳大利亞頭巾式海螺的殼可以用來做襯衫的亮鈕子。
15. 很多人，尤其是法國人，認為花園裏的蝸牛 escargot 是一道美食。
16. 蝸牛可以活 2-20 年。

给小朋友
有关蚂蚁和蜗牛的有趣常识

蚂蚁

1. 蚂蚁是群居的昆虫。它们住在有组织的社区，叫做群居蚂蚁窝。
2. 蚂蚁有两万二千种。多数都是暗色，像黑色、棕色、褐色，有的是黄色、绿色、蓝色、或紫色。
3. 蚂蚁建造很多不同样子的蚂蚁窝。有些种类把窝建在地下，在泥土里挖穴道和房间。
4. 一个蚂蚁窝可能有几打、几百，几千或几百万只蚂蚁。每一个群居窝里有一只或好几只蚂蚁皇后。
5. 蚂蚁皇后的主要工作就是生蛋，她一生可以生几千个蛋。她们比工蚁大好几倍。蚂蚁皇后可以活 10-30 年。
6. 蚂蚁窝里多数的蚂蚁是工蚁，像蚂蚁皇后一样，都是母的（雌蚁）。工蚁建造蚂蚁窝、寻找食物、照顾宝宝、和敌人打仗。体型最大的工蚁叫做兵蚁，它们的头比一般工蚁大。工蚁能活一年以下到五年以上。
7. 公的蚂蚁（雄蚁）在蚂蚁窝里不做任何事。它们唯一的工作是和年轻的蚂蚁皇后交配。在它们做交配飞行之前只活几个星期或几个月。交配之后，它们不久就死了。它们也比工蚁大。

8. 不同种类的蚂蚁有不同的尺寸，但是大部分体型都很小。最小的蚂蚁只有 1/25 英寸（0.1 公分）长。最大的蚂蚁有一英寸（0.1 公分）（2.公分）长。

9. 蚂蚁非常强壮。多数的蚂蚁可以抬动比它身体重10倍的东西。有些蚂蚁可以抬动重50倍的东西。

10. 蚂蚁有很有趣的身体。一只蚂蚁头有两根长满细毛和小刺的触角、一对（两个）多镜头的复眼、和一对（两个）多功能的颚。

11. 蚂蚁用它们的触角嗅闻其他的蚂蚁。这样它们能认得同窝的蚂蚁。触角是蚂蚁触觉、味觉、听觉、和嗅觉的器官。

12. 蚂蚁在它张开嘴巴的下面有一个小的食物袋。同窝的蚂蚁把食物吐出来分享食物。两只蚂蚁嘴对嘴站着，一只把食物吐一些给另外的一只吃。全蚂蚁窝的蚂蚁都分享食物。

13. 一只蚂蚁有三对（六只）脚长在身体的下面。每一只脚有9节，由可以弯曲的关节连着。

14. 蚂蚁每一只前脚有两个梳子，像颚上的梳子一样，来清洁其他的脚和触角。

15. 大多种类的蚂蚁，公蚁（雄蚁）和小皇后有两对翅膀长在身体上。它们只在交配时用一次翅膀。工蚁没有翅膀。

16. 蚂蚁的成长有四个阶段：（1）卵，（2）幼虫，（3）蛹，（4）成虫。

17. 蜘蛛、青蛙、蛤蟆、四脚蛇、鸟、和很多种的昆虫都吃蚂蚁。蚂蚁用叮咬来抵抗敌人保护自己。过半数的蚂蚁有叮刺，有些还能喷毒液。

18. 不同蚂蚁窝的工蚁在见面时，会常常打仗。有些蚂蚁打仗激烈造成死亡。得胜者会侵犯打败者的蚂蚁窝，把幼蚁带走当食物。

19. 蚂蚁用散发的化学分泌物和别的蚂蚁沟通。这些化学分泌物是从头部、身体、尾部的腺体分泌。这些化学分泌物有蚂蚁敏感的特殊气味。不同种的化学分泌物表达不同的资讯，有如"发现食物"和"危险讯号"。

20. 蚂蚁用气味分辨同窝蚂蚁或敌人。当两只蚂蚁碰面时，它们用触角嗅闻对方。如果它们是同窝的，两只蚂蚁就站着嘴对嘴，一只蚂蚁就把一滴食物吐到另一只蚂蚁的嘴里。

21. 蚂蚁在自然生态平衡上扮演重要的角色。它们吃大量的昆虫，不让昆虫繁殖得太多。蚂蚁也是鸟儿、青蛙、四脚蛇和许多动物的食物。

22. 蚂蚁对农人有益也有害。有些蚂蚁吃损害农作物的害虫，帮助农人。有些蚂蚁在地下挖掘蚂蚁窝，把泥土散开、挖松、混合，对农人有益。

23. 有些蚂蚁保护伤害农作物的害虫，对农人有害。他们也会叮人咬人，引起人类敏感。

24. 很多种类的蚂蚁是家里的害虫，它们咬穿木梁侵犯房屋、饭店、医院、谷仓、还吃存放的食物。

25. 在用喷雾杀虫剂驱除蚂蚁之前，一定要确认那杀虫剂是安全有效。用柠檬汁和白醋抹在蚂蚁走道上是安全的。

26. 有很多文化用蚂蚁做菜或医病。

27. 在南极、格林兰岛、冰岛、波里尼西亚和夏威夷一部分的岛没有土生的蚂蚁。

28. 蚂蚁化石说明蚂蚁在地球上已经有一亿年（100,000,000）了。

29. 在非洲发现9500万年前最古老的琥珀化石中有28种昆虫，其中一只像蚂蚁。

蜗牛（螺）

1. 蜗牛是一种动物，它的软身体有一个壳盖住。
2. 它的身体有一个有触角的头、眼睛、一张嘴、和小牙齿。
3. 蜗牛用叫做脚的强壮肌肉爬行。
4. 一只在爬行的蜗牛大量分泌粘液造成一条狭路好滑行。天气乾燥的时候，蜗牛用乾的粘液，造成一个门，把自己关在自己的壳子里面，在不动的情况下休息，等待乾季结束。
5. 世界上已经有8万（80,000）种蜗牛——有些像针头一样小，有些有两尺（61公分）长。
6. 什么地方都有蜗牛：在陆地上、在淡水中（河、池、湖、温泉）、和海洋里。
7. 住在陆地上的蜗牛是雌雄同体（在身体里有雌性和雄性器官）。大部分的陆地蜗牛有肺。
8. 大部分住在水里的蜗牛，不是雌的，就是雄的。（不是雌雄同体。）
9. 有些淡水蜗牛有肺，必需浮到水面来呼吸空气中的氧气。有些淡水蜗牛有鳃，可以吸取水中的氧气。
10. 咸水（海洋）里的蜗牛（海螺）是最多的蜗牛——有5万5千种住在海岸边或深海的海底。大部分有鳃。
11. 陆地上的蜗牛损坏花朵、蔬菜、和植物。但是很多蜗牛是鸟儿的好食物。
12. 有些印度洋和太平洋西南方的蜗牛（海螺）有毒刺，可以杀死小鱼，也造成人类的死亡。
13. 有些从污染的淡水和海洋里的蜗牛（螺）带病菌，人不能吃。
14. 澳大利亚头巾式海螺的壳可以用来做衬衫的亮扣子。
15. 很多人，尤其是法国人，认为花园里的蜗牛 escargot 是一道美食。
16. 蜗牛可以活2-20年。

Ant & Snail Workshop for Children

1. Find some ants and snails near your home. *Observe* their *behavior*. Tell your family or teacher about what you *observe*.

2. Do you like ants and snails? Tell your family or teacher why or why not.

3. Collect some beautiful shells of ocean snails. Would you like to *decorate* your home with the *colorful* shells?

4. Draw some sea snails and *color* them.

5. Go to the library, or check the *internet* to find out the interesting *characteristics* about different groups of ants: (1) army ants, (2) slave makers, (3) *harvester* ants, (4) *dairying* ants, (5) honey ants, (6) *fungus* growers.

6. Please tell your family or friends why ants are Important in the *balance* of nature.

7. Make a *Home-Made* Ant Farm
   Making an ant farm with your child is a fun project. Here are instructions on how to make a *homemade* ant farm.

You'll Need:
- Large Glass Jar
- PVC Pipe
- Dirt
- Ants
- Brown Paper Bag

Directions:

- Cut a piece of PVC pipe to fit inside the glass jar, while still *allowing* you to close the jar. Find an *anthill* and use a *shovel* to *scoop* ants and dirt and fill the jar.
- Put your little home-made ant farm into the brown paper bag for a week to *encourage* the ants to build their *tunnels* right along the side of the glass jar.

To feed your ants, drop some *breadcrumbs* and tiny pieces of fruit and vegetable in the jar.

To provide your ants with water, drop a moist cotton ball in the jar.

給小朋友
螞蟻和蝸牛的工作室

1. 在你家的附近找一些螞蟻和蝸牛。觀察它們的行動。告訴你的家人或老師,你看到了什麼。

2. 你喜歡螞蟻和蝸牛嗎?告訴你的家人或老師,你為什麼喜歡或不喜歡。

3. 收集一些美麗的海螺貝殼。你喜不喜歡用海螺貝殼裝飾你的家呢?

4. 畫一些海螺,再塗上顏色。

5. 去圖書館或上網查一查有關不同種類的螞蟻的有趣特性:(1)軍隊螞蟻,(2)奴隸螞蟻,(3)收穫螞蟻,(4)奶品螞蟻(5)蜜糖螞蟻,(6)生產菌類的螞蟻。

6. 請告訴你的家人或朋友,為什麼螞蟻在自然生態平衡上很重要。

8. 做一個螞蟻窩:和孩子做一個螞蟻窩是個有趣的活動。方法如下:

必需品: 大的玻璃罐、PVC朔料管、土、螞蟻、牛皮紙購物袋

方法: 切一段PVC朔料管剛好放在大玻璃罐中,罐子仍能蓋上。蓋子上打幾個小洞。找一個螞蟻窩,用鏟子把螞蟻和土填入玻璃罐,大約2/3滿。

把自製的螞蟻窩放在牛皮紙購物袋中等一星期,讓螞蟻在玻璃罐內沿邊造地道。

放些麵包屑、小片水果或蔬菜餵螞蟻。丟一個濕的棉花球在玻璃罐裏給螞蟻喝水。

给小朋友：
蚂蚁和蜗牛的工作室

1. 在你家的附近找一些蚂蚁和蜗牛。观察它们的行动。告诉你的家人或老师，你看到了什么。

2. 你喜欢蚂蚁和蜗牛吗？告诉你的家人或老师，你为什么喜欢或不喜欢。

3. 收集一些美丽的海螺贝壳。你喜不喜欢用海螺贝壳装饰你的家呢？

4. 画一些海螺，再涂上颜色。

5. 去图书馆或上网查一查有关不同重类的蚂蚁的有趣特性：（1）军队蚂蚁，（2）奴隶蚂蚁，（3）收获蚂蚁，（4）奶品蚂蚁，（5）蜜糖蚂蚁，（6）生产菌类的蚂蚁。

6. 请告诉你的家人或朋友，为什么蚂蚁在自然生态平衡上很重要。

7. 做一个蚂蚁窝：和孩子做一个蚂蚁窝是个有趣的活动。方法如下：

必需品：大的玻璃罐、PVC朔料管、土、蚂蚁、牛皮纸购物袋

方法：切一段PVC朔料管刚好放在大玻璃罐中，罐子仍能盖上。盖子上打几个小洞。找一个蚂蚁窝，用铲子把蚂蚁和土填入玻璃罐，大约2/3满。

把自制的蚂蚁窝放在牛皮纸购物袋中等一星期，让蚂蚁在玻璃罐内沿边造地道。

放些面包屑、小片水果或蔬菜喂蚂蚁。丢一个湿的棉花球在玻璃罐里给蚂蚁喝水。

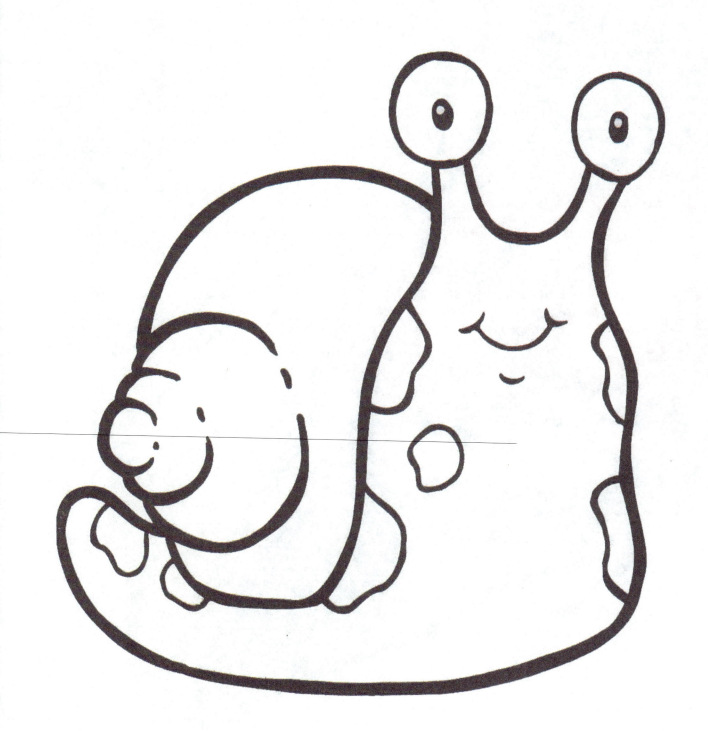

Ladybugs

小瓢蟲
xiǎo piáo chóng
小瓢虫

Mildred Shaw & Dr. Loretta Huang 杜英慈
Illustrated by Tiffany Hayashi 绘图

Ladybugs

小瓢蟲
xiǎo piáo chóng
小瓢虫

A little Ladybug am I
With tiny wings so I can fly.
I have a coat that is bright red;
I'm easily seen in a garden bed.
I love to eat aphids and mites,
But I don't buzz, or sting, or bite.
I'm only about the size of a pea,
And my little red body is nice to see.
I have many dots of black
Scattered on my bright red back.
People say I'm cute and neat;
Seeing me is quite a treat.

Tiny wings from my back appear;
They help me fly not far but near.
People want us in their yard
As Because we work so very hard.
Ladybugs are a gardener's friend;
On us, you can truly depend.
We don't like insecticide spray;
A whiff of that will end our day.
If you should need us more and more,
Please buy us at the garden store.
It's wonderful what we can do,
Feeding ourselves while helping you.

Words of wisdom:

Keep a green tree in your heart, and perhaps a singing bird will come.

智慧之語：心中有綠樹，鳴鳥自然來。
zhì huì zhī yǔ　xīn zhōng yǒu lǜ shù　míng niǎo zì rán lái
智慧之语：心中有绿树，鸣鸟自然来。

"Ladybugs"

A little Ladybug am I
With tiny wings so I can fly.

小ㄒㄧㄠˇ瓢ㄆㄧㄠˊ蟲ㄔㄨㄥˊ

我ㄨㄛˇ是ㄕˋ一ㄧ隻ㄓ小ㄒㄧㄠˇ瓢ㄆㄧㄠˊ蟲ㄔㄨㄥˊ

我ㄨㄛˇ有ㄧㄡˇ小ㄒㄧㄠˇ翅ㄔˋ膀ㄅㄤˇ我ㄨㄛˇ能ㄋㄥˊ飛ㄈㄟ。

xiǎo piáo chóng
小 瓢 虫

wǒ shì yī zhǐ xiǎo piáo chóng
我 是 一 只 小 瓢 虫 ,

wǒ yǒu xiǎo chì bǎng wǒ néng fēi
我 有 小 翅 膀 我 能 飞 。

Ladybugs

I have a coat that is bright red;
I'm easily seen in a garden bed.

我有鮮紅色的大衣；
容易在花園中被看見。

wǒ yǒu xiān hóng sè di dà yī
我有鲜红色的大衣；
róng yì zài huā yuán zhōng bèi kàn jiàn
容易在花园中被看见。

Ladybugs

I love to eat aphids and mites,
But I don't buzz, or sting, or bite.

我愛吃小蟲和蚜蟲，

但是我不嗡嗡叫、叮人、或咬人。

wǒ ài chī xiǎo chóng hé yá chóng
我爱吃小虫和蚜虫，
dàn shì wǒ bù wēng wēng jiào dīng rén huò yǎo rén
但是我不嗡嗡叫、叮人、或咬人。

111

Ladybugs

I'm only about the size of a pea,
And my little red body is nice to see.

我ㄨㄛˇ只ㄓˇ有ㄧㄡˇ豌ㄨㄢ豆ㄉㄡˋ的ㄉㄜ˙大ㄉㄚˋ小ㄒㄧㄠˇ，

我ㄨㄛˇ的ㄉㄜ˙小ㄒㄧㄠˇ紅ㄏㄨㄥˊ身ㄕㄣ體ㄊㄧˇ很ㄏㄣˇ好ㄏㄠˇ看ㄎㄢˋ（瞧ㄑㄧㄠˊ）。

wǒ zhǐ yǒu wān dòu dì dà xiǎo
我 只 有 豌 豆 的 大 小 ，
wǒ dì xiǎo hóng shēn tǐ hěn hǎo kàn (qiáo)
我 的 小 红 身 体 很 好 看 （瞧）。

Ladybugs

I have many dots of black
Scattered on my bright red back.

我有很多黑點點

散佈在我鮮紅的背上。

wǒ yǒu hěn duō hēi diǎn diǎn
我有很多黑点点
sàn bù zài wǒ xiān hóng dí bèi shàng
散布在我鲜红的背上。

People say I'm cute and neat;
Seeing me is quite a treat.

人們說我可愛又整潔；
看見我真是快樂的好事。

rén men shuō wǒ kě ài yòu zhěng jié
人们说我可爱又整洁；
kàn jiàn wǒ zhēn shì kuài lè de hǎo shì
看见我真是快乐的好事。

Ladybugs

Tiny wings from my back appear;
They help me fly not far but near.

小小翅膀長在我的背上,
幫助我飛到近處但是不能飛翔到遠處。

xiǎo xiǎo chì bǎng cháng zài wǒ dí bèi shàng
小小翅膀长在我的背上,
bāng zhù wǒ fēi dào jìn chù dàn shì bù néng fēi xiáng dào yuǎn chù
帮助我飞到近处但是不能飞翔到远处。

People want us in their yard
Because we work so very hard.

人人都要我們在他們的院子裏
因為我們工作得很努力。

rén rén dū yào wǒ men zài tā men dí yuàn zǐ lǐ
人人都要我们在他们的院子里
yīn wéi wǒ men dí gōng zuò dé hěn nǔ lì
因为我们的工作得很努力，

Ladybugs

Ladybugs are a gardener's friend;
On us, you can truly depend.

瓢ㄆㄧㄠˊ蟲ㄔㄨㄥˊ是ㄕˋ園ㄩㄢˊ丁ㄉㄧㄥ的ㄉㄜ˙朋ㄆㄥˊ友ㄧㄡˇ；
你ㄋㄧˇ可ㄎㄜˇ以ㄧˇ真ㄓㄣ正ㄓㄥˋ地ㄉㄧˋ信ㄒㄧㄣˋ任ㄖㄣˋ我ㄨㄛˇ們ㄇㄣ˙。

piáo chóng shì yuán dīng di péng yǒu
瓢 虫 是 园 丁 的 朋 友；
nǐ kě yǐ zhēn zhèng di xìn rèn wǒ men
你 可 以 真 正 地 信 任 我 们。

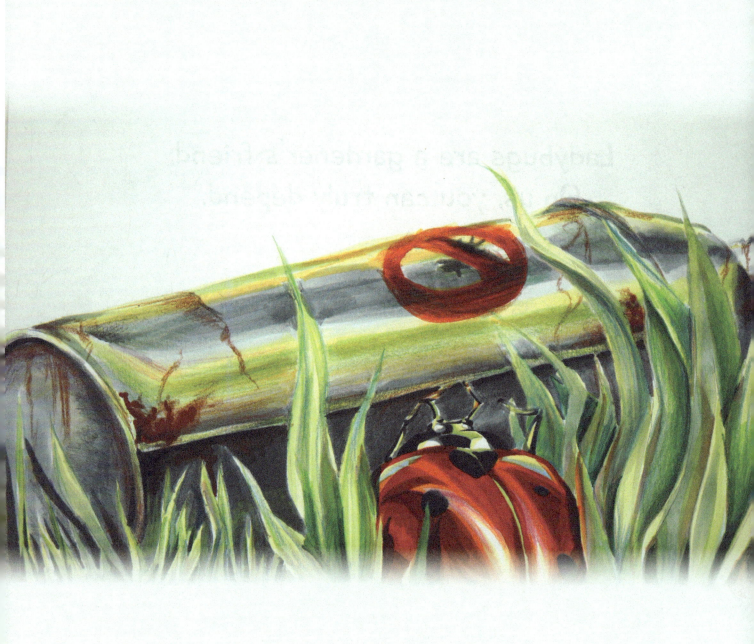

Ladybugs

We don't like insecticide spray;
A whiff of that will end our day.

我們不喜歡殺蟲噴霧；
噴一下我們就死了。

wǒ men bù xǐ huān shā chóng pēn wù
我们不喜欢杀虫喷雾；
pēn yī xià wǒ men jiù sǐ liǎo
喷一下我们就死了。

Ladybugs

If you should need us more and more,
Please buy us at the garden store.

假如你需要更多更多的瓢蟲,
請到園藝商店裏買我們。

jiǎ rú nǐ xū yào gēng duō gēng duō di piáo chóng
假如你需要更多更多的瓢虫,
qǐng dào yuán yì shāng diàn lǐ mǎi wǒ men
请到园艺商店里买我们。

It's wonderful what we can do,
Feeding ourselves while helping you.

我們能做太美妙的事,
喂飽自己同時也幫助你。

wǒ men néng zuò tài měi miào di shì
我们能做太美妙的事,
wèi bǎo zì jǐ tóng shí yě bāng zhù nǐ
喂饱自己同时也帮助你。

To Children — Interesting Facts about "Ladybugs"

1. Is the ladybug a *harmful* or helpful insect for the garden? **(Helpful in general)**

2. How are they helpful? **(They eat the garden pests such as *mites, aphids*.)**

3. What are other names for the ladybug? **(Ladybird, ladybird beetle, lady beetle, lucky bug)**

4. What colors can ladybugs be? **(Red, yellow, orange, brown, and black)**

5. What is the shape of a ladybug? **(Round, or oval-shaped)**

6. If you were to compare a ladybug's size to something, what would it be? **(Peas, *approximately* 1/4 inch)**

7. Do all ladybugs have spots? **(No, some do not have spots at all.)** Look at your ladybugs. Can you see any of them that do not have any spots?

8. What is the ladybug's life *cycle*? Does it go through *metamorphosis* like butterflies, or do they just hatch out of eggs as mini ladybugs? **(They go through metamorphosis--egg, larvae, pupa, adult.)**

9. Where do you usually find them in the garden? **(Where the pests are, rose buds, leaves)**

10. What type of bug is the ladybug? (A. spider **B. beetle** C. moth D. butterfly)

11. What do ladybugs eat? **(Aphids, *mites*, scale insects, meal bugs)** Those are common garden pests.

12. Guess how many aphids a larva eats in a day. **(20-30).** How many can adults eat? **(Over 50)**

13. How many eggs can a ladybug lay each time? **(3-300 eggs)**

14. When a ladybug flies, how many times does it beat its wings per second? **(85 times per second)**

15. Can ladybugs be (A. Red with black dots B. Black with red dots **C. both**)

16. Who is the ladybug's *major predator*? **(Birds)**

17. How do the ladybugs *defend* themselves from their *predators*? **(bright color, playing dead, bad taste)**

18. Where are the ladybug's wings located? **(On the back, protected by a pair of shells)**

19. How many legs does a ladybug have? **(6)**

20. Do ladybugs have *antennae*? **(Yes)**

21. Are the spots on the ladybug's back *symmetrical or random*? **(Random)**

22. Recently, people are using bug spray to kill off pests. Why is this choice not as good as using ladybugs? **(Because bug spray kills good and bad insects. Ladybugs eat only pests.)**

23. The Asian ladybug (called *harmonia axyridis*) is not so cute. **(It bites.)** Check out http://www.cirrusimage.com/beetles_ladybird.htm.

24. How long can an adult ladybug live? **(A few weeks up to a year)**

25. Have ladybugs traveled into space? **(Yes. Four ladybugs and a jar of aphids were carried on a space shuttle as part of a zero gravity test to study their movement. Ladybugs were able to capture their prey without the help of gravity!)**

26. Ladybugs are *considered* good luck. **(True, also called lucky bugs)**

給小朋友
有關小瓢蟲的趣味知識

1. 小瓢蟲是園子裏的害蟲還是益蟲？（益蟲。）
2. 它為什麼是益蟲呢？（它吃園子裏的害蟲。）
4. 小瓢蟲有什麼其他的英文名字？(ladybird, ladybird beetle, lady beetle, lucky bug)
5. 小瓢蟲是什麼顏色？（有紅色，黃色，橘色，棕色，和黑色。）
6. 小瓢蟲是什麼形狀？（圓形或橢圓形。）
7. 假如你把瓢蟲和一樣東西比較，它的大小像什麼？（像豌豆，大約 1/4 英吋。）
8. 所有的小瓢蟲都有點點嗎？（有的沒有點點。）看看你的小瓢蟲，有沒有點點？
9. 小瓢蟲的生命循環是什麼？是不是它們和蝴蝶一樣從卵變成幼蟲，再變成繭，最後是成蟲？或是它們從卵就直接孵化成小瓢蟲？（卵，幼蟲，繭，成蟲。）
10. 你在園子裏什麼地方會找到小瓢蟲？（在有害蟲的地方，像玫瑰花苞和葉子上。）
11. 小瓢蟲是那一種蟲子？（是一種甲蟲。）
12. 小瓢蟲吃什麼？（它們吃園子裏一般的小害蟲。）
13. 猜一猜：小瓢蟲的幼蟲一天吃幾隻小害蟲？（大約 20-30 隻；成蟲一天吃 50 隻以上。）瓢蟲一次生幾個蛋？（3-300 個）
14. 瓢蟲飛的時候，每秒鐘拍動翅膀幾次？（每秒鐘拍動翅膀 85 次。）
15. 小瓢蟲是否可以紅色帶黑點或黑色帶紅點？（兩種都有。）

16. 誰是小瓢蟲的敵人？（鳥兒們。）

17. 小瓢蟲怎麼樣保護自己？（鮮麗的顏色，裝死，不好吃的味道。）

18. 小瓢蟲的翅膀長在那兒？（長在背上，有一對副翅保護著。）

19. 小瓢蟲有幾隻腳呀？（六隻。）

20. 小瓢蟲有觸角嗎？（有兩個。）

21. 小瓢蟲身上的點點是對稱的還是不規則的？（是不規則的。）

22. 近來，有許多人用殺蟲劑驅除害蟲。為什麼這方法不如用瓢蟲驅除害蟲好？（因為殺蟲劑把害蟲和益蟲都殺死了。小瓢蟲只吃害蟲。）

23. 有一種亞洲瓢蟲不太可愛。它會咬人。請上網查 http://www.cirrusimage.com/beetles_ladybird.htm

24. 瓢蟲能活多久？（幾周、幾個月、不超過一年。）

25. 瓢蟲登上太空了嗎？（是的。四隻瓢蟲和一罐蚜蟲被帶到太空艙裏，研究它們在太空無重情況下的行動。瓢蟲在無重環境中也能抓到蚜蟲吃。）

26. 人們認為瓢蟲帶來好運嗎？（是的。瓢蟲也叫做"好運蟲"。）

给小朋友
有关小瓢虫的趣味知识

1. 小瓢虫是园子里的害虫还是益虫？（益虫。）
2. 它为什么是益虫呢？（它吃园子里的害虫。）
3. 小瓢虫有什么其他的英文名字？（ladybird, ladybird beetle, lady beetle, lucky bug）
4. 小瓢虫是什么颜色？（有红色，黄色，橘色，棕色，和黑色。）
5. 小瓢虫是什么形状？（圆形或椭圆形。）
6. 假如你把小瓢虫和一样东西比较，它的大小像什么？（像豌豆，大约1/4英寸。）
7. 所有的小瓢虫都有点点吗？（有的没有点点。）看看你的小瓢虫，有没有点点？
8. 小瓢虫的生命循环是什么？是不是它们和蝴蝶一样从卵变成幼虫，再变成茧，最后是成虫？或是它们从卵就直接孵化成小瓢虫？（卵，幼虫，茧，成虫。）

9. 你在园子里什么地方会找到小瓢虫？（在有害虫的地方，像玫瑰花苞和叶子上。）
10. 小瓢虫是那一种虫子？（是一种甲虫。）
11. 小瓢虫吃什么？（它们吃园子里的一般小害虫。）
12. 猜一猜：小瓢虫的幼虫一天吃几只小害虫？（大约20-30只；成虫一天吃50只以上。）
13. 瓢虫一次生几个蛋？（3-300个）
14. 瓢虫飞的时候，每秒钟拍动翅膀几次？（每秒钟拍动翅膀85次。）
15. 小瓢虫是否可以红色带黑点或黑色带红点？（两种都有。）

16. 谁是小瓢虫的敌人？（鸟儿们。）

17. 小瓢虫怎么样保护自己？（鲜丽的颜色，装死，不好吃的味道。）

18. 小瓢虫的翅膀长在那儿？（长在背上，有一对副翅保护著。）

19. 小瓢虫有几只脚呀？（六只。）

20. 小瓢虫有触角吗？（有两个。）

21. 小瓢虫身上的点点是对称的还是不规则的？（是不规则的。）

22. 近来，有许多人用杀虫剂驱除害虫。为什么这方法不如用瓢虫驱除害虫好？（因为杀虫剂把害虫和益虫都杀死了。小瓢虫只吃害虫。）

23. 有一种亚洲瓢虫不太可爱。它会咬人。请上网查 http://www.cirrusimage.com/beetles_ladybird.htm

24. 瓢虫能活多久？（几周、几个月、不超过一年。）

25. 瓢虫登上太空了吗？（是的。四只瓢虫和一罐蚜虫被带到太空舱里，研究它们在太空无重情况下的行动。瓢虫在无重环境中也能抓到蚜虫吃。）

26. 人们认为瓢虫带来好运吗。（是的。瓢虫也叫做"好运虫"。）

Ladybug Workshops
Ladybugs-In-A-Cup

How to make:

1. Put ladybugs in the fridge overnight. (Don't worry. They hibernate!)
2. Put foliage (leaves, flowers, sticks) into a clear plastic cup.
3. For moisture, place 1-2 cotton balls into each cup.
4. Take out ladybugs, put them into cups QUICKLY! They WILL fly/crawl everywhere once they wake up!
5. Tightly seal over the cups with plastic wrap, use rubber bands or tape just in case.
6. Poke holes with toothpick into plastic wrap to circulate oxygen in cups.
7. Enjoy. After a few days, release ladybugs in yard so they will not die.
8. If giving away, tell keepers to release them in the backyard.

Preparing ladybugs—they get everywhere!

Did you know they can live in the fridge?

Close-up of cups without ladybugs

Close up proof! They are alive and crawl

Cookies

How to make:

1. Bake sugar cookies according to instructions. (We recommend Betty Crocker brand.)
2. Take vanilla frosting; drip copious amounts of red food coloring in. Mix frosting until it turns into a deep red color.
3. Spread a thick layer of frosting over the sugar cookie.
4. Squeeze a line of black decoration frosting across the center of cookie.
5. Add Reese© as head: add M&M's© as spots.
6. It's ready to eat with lots and lots of milk!
7. If any leftovers, put in the fridge for an hour in container or on plate with plastic wrap.

Take sugar cookies out of oven...

Packed into container.

All done!

Finished cookie. must. Resist. Eating.

Ladybug Magnets

How to make:

1. Use red spray paint to color glass marbles red. Wait 15-20 minutes to dry.
2. Using black permanent marker, draw dots, head, and shell.
3. Using super glue (by adults), glue magnets on backside of glass marbles. Wait for 20-30 minutes to dry.
4. Glue on wiggle eyes and string antenna, using small dabs of superglue.
5. The ladybugs are done!

Spray-painted glass marbles

Many, many ladybugs

Glue on magnet to backside

Add on eyes and antenna, done!

瓢蟲工作室
瓢蟲花杯

1. 把瓢蟲盒子放在冰箱裏。（別擔心，它們會在低溫裏睡覺。）
2. 把葉子、花、小枝放在透明的塑膠杯子裏。
3. 每一個杯子裏放兩個濕棉花球，保持杯子裏的濕度。
4. 把瓢蟲盒子拿出來。快快把瓢蟲放進塑膠杯子裏！它們一醒來就會到處飛到處爬了！
5. 用保鮮膜把杯子口緊緊地包起。用橡皮筋或膠帶匝緊杯口。
6. 用牙籤把保鮮膜扎幾個洞，讓杯子裏的空氣流通。
7. 欣賞你的瓢蟲花杯。幾天後，把瓢蟲放生在花園中。否則瓢蟲會死掉。
8. 假如你把花杯送給小朋友，告訴他一定要把瓢蟲放生在後院裏。

瓢蟲點心

1. 按照烘烤糖餅干的步驟烘烤糖餅干。（我們建議用 Betty Crocker 的牌子）。
2. 用香草口味的糖霜加上紅色食品顏料。攪拌糖霜至深紅色。
3. 把紅色糖霜厚厚一層塗抹在烤好的餅干上。（不愛吃甜的小朋友，不要塗太厚。）
4. 擠一條黑色的糖霜在餅干的中線上。
5. 把 Reese 花生醬夾心的圓巧克力放在餅干上當瓢蟲頭，M&M 小巧克力當瓢蟲身上的點點。
6. 現在可以吃瓢蟲餅干和喝大量的牛奶一塊兒當點心。
7. 如果有剩下的餅干，用保鮮膜包好或裝入盒子，放在冰箱裏，以後再吃。

瓢虫吸鐵石裝飾

1. 用紅色噴漆把扁平玻璃珠噴成紅色。等15-20分鐘乾燥。
2. 用不退色黑色馬克筆畫黑點點，頭，和虫殼。
3. 用強力膠把小吸鐵石粘在玻璃的背面。等20-30分鐘讓它乾燥。
4. 用一丁點兒強力膠把活動眼珠和細觸角粘在紅身體上。
5. 瓢虫裝飾就完成了！

瓢虫工作室

瓢虫花杯

1. 把瓢虫盒子放在冰箱里。（别担心，它们会在低温里睡觉。）
2. 把叶子、花、小枝放在透明的塑胶杯子里。
3. 一个杯子里放一两个湿棉花球保持杯子里的湿度。
4. 把瓢虫盒子拿出来。快快把瓢虫放进塑胶杯子里！它们一醒来就会到处飞到处爬了！
5. 用保鲜膜把杯子口紧紧包起。用橡皮筋或胶带匝紧杯口。
6. 用牙签把保鲜膜扎几个洞，让杯子里的空气流通。
7. 欣赏你的瓢虫花杯。几天后，把瓢虫放生在花园中。否则瓢虫会死掉。
8. 假如你把花杯送给小朋友，告诉他一定要把瓢虫放生在后院里。

瓢虫点心

1. 按照烘烤糖饼干的步骤烘烤糖饼干。(我们建议用Betty Crocker的牌子)。
2. 用香草口味的糖霜加上红色食品颜料。搅拌糖霜至深红色。
3. 把红色糖霜厚厚一层涂抹在烤好的饼干上。(不爱吃甜的小朋友,不要涂太厚。)
4. 挤一条黑色的糖霜在饼干的中线上。
5. 把Reese花生酱夹心的园巧克力放上,当瓢虫头。M&M小巧克力当瓢虫身上的点点。
6. 现在可以吃瓢虫饼干和喝大量的牛奶一块儿当点心。
7. 如果有剩下的饼干,用保鲜膜包好或装入盒子,放在冰箱里,以后再吃。

瓢虫吸铁石装饰

1. 用红色喷漆把扁平玻璃珠喷成红色。等15-20分钟乾燥。
2. 用不退色黑色马克笔画黑点点,头,和虫壳。
3. 用强力胶把小吸铁石粘在玻璃的背面。等20-30分钟让它乾燥。
4. 用一丁点儿强力胶把活动眼珠和细触角粘在红身体上。
5. 瓢虫装饰就完成了!

The Life and Times of Baby Robins

知ㄓ 更ㄍㄥ 鳥ㄋㄧㄠˇ 寶ㄅㄠˇ 寶ㄅㄠˇ 的ㄉㄜ˙ 一ㄧ 生ㄕㄥ

zhī gēng niǎo bǎo bǎo dì yī shēng
知更鸟宝宝的一生

Mildred Shaw & Dr. Loretta Huang 杜 _{dù yīng cí} 英慈

Illustrated by Gina Chang 张 _{zhāng yàn jùn} 彦珺

Life and Times of Baby Robins

知更鳥寶寶的一生
zhī gēng niǎo bǎo bǎo dì yī shēng
知更鸟宝宝的一生

High up in a tree is Mother Robin Red Breast;
And in that tree she has made a really neat nest.
Perched in that nest are her tiny birds three;
They are all as hungry as they can be.
This hungry brood of three sits chirping
in their nest;
They seldom give their mother bird some time
to rest.
Beneath the tree is a yard with grass so green;
Mother Robin knows that worms can
soon be seen.
Sprinklers appear as cold water they spray,
They make worms crawl out to greet
the wet day.
Mother Robin waits for worms to appear;
Then she can see that a good meal is near.
On the grass she searches with her keen eyes.
She grabs wiggly worms that she quickly spies
A fat, juicy worm only makes a tiny bite,
For hungry baby birds with a huge appetite.

Mother grabs as much food as her bill will hold,
Then feeds her babies and protects them
from the cold.

Then the babies' feathers begin to grow;
Mother must work harder than they'll ever know.
The babies' wingspans begin to expand,
And mother bird will soon surely demand,
That these baby birds must now learn to fly;
It won't be long before they wave good-bye.
Flying a short distance to close twigs
and branches,
Baby birds are soon making big advances.
A few more days of worms, bugs, and seeds,
Will take good care of these growing
birds' needs.
Now adults, the young birds wave
a cheerful good-bye,
Mother Robin says farewell with a chirping sigh.

Words of wisdom:

Honor your parents.

智慧之語： 孝敬父母
zhì huì zhī yǔ xiào jìng fù mǔ
智慧之语：孝敬父母

Life and Times of Baby Robins

High up in a tree is Mother Robin Red Breast;
And in that tree she has made a really neat nest.

知更鳥寶寶的一生

高高的樹上有隻紅胸脯知更鳥媽媽；
在樹上她造了一個真乾淨的家。

zhī gēng niǎo bǎo bǎo di yī shēng
知更鸟宝宝的一生

gāo gāo di shù shàng yǒu zhī hóng xiōng fú zhī gēng niǎo mā mā
高高的树上有只红胸脯知更鸟妈妈；
zài shù shàng tā zào liǎo yī gè zhēn qián jìng di jiā
在树上她造了一个真乾净的家。

The Life and Times of Baby Robins

Perched in that nest are her tiny birds three;
They are all as hungry as they can be.

鳥窩裏棲息著三隻小小鳥；
它們都餓得不得了。

niǎo wō lǐ qī xī zhù sān zhǐ xiǎo xiǎo niǎo
鸟窝里栖息著三只小小鸟；
tā men dū è dé bù dé liǎo
它们都饿得不得了。

The Life and Times of Baby Robins

This hungry brood of three sits
chirping in their nest;
They seldom give their mother bird
some time to rest.

這一窩飢餓的三隻小鳥啾啾叫著
坐在鳥巢裏；
它們很少給媽媽一點時間休息。

这一窝饥饿的三只小鸟啾啾叫著坐在鸟巢里；
它们很少给妈妈一点时间休息。

Beneath the tree is a yard
with grass so green;
Mother Robin knows that worms
can soon be seen.

樹下有一個綠草院；
知更鳥媽媽知道蟲子很快就會被看見。

shù xià yǒu yī gè lù cǎo yuàn
树下有一个绿草院；
zhī gēng niǎo mā mā zhī dào chóng zǐ hěn kuài jiù huì bèi kàn jiàn
知更鸟妈妈知道虫子很快就会被看见。

The Life and Times of Baby Robins

Sprinklers appear as cold water they spray,
They make worms crawl out to greet
the wet day.

當冷水噴出， 噴水器就跳起出現，
讓蟲子爬出來歡迎等待潮濕的一天。

dāng lěng shuǐ pēn chū　　pēn shuǐ qì jiù tiào qǐ chū xiàn
当冷水喷出，喷水器就跳起出现，
ràng chóng zǐ pá chū lái huān yíng děng dài cháo shī dì yī tiān
让虫子爬出来欢迎等待潮湿的一天。

Mother Robin waits for worms to appear;
Then she can see that a good meal is near.

知更鳥媽媽等候蟲子出現；
然後她能看到美味餐點很快就呈現。

zhī gēng niǎo mā mā děng hòu chóng zǐ chū xiàn
知更鸟妈妈等候虫子出现；
rán hòu tā néng kàn dào měi wèi cān diǎn hěn kuài jiù chéng xiàn
然後她能看到美味餐点很快就呈现。

The Life and Times of Baby Robins

On the grass she searches
with her keen eyes.
She grabs wiggly worms
that she quickly spies.

她用敏鋭的眼睛搜尋著草坪。
她快速地抓起立即看到的蠕動的蚯蚓。

tā yòng mǐn ruì dí yǎn jīng sōu xún zhuó cǎo píng
她用敏锐的眼睛搜寻着草坪。
tā kuài sù dì zhuā qǐ lì jí kàn dào dí rú dòng dí qiū yǐn
她快速地抓起立即看到的蠕动的蚯蚓。

The Life and Times of Baby Robins

A fat, juicy worm only makes a tiny bite,
For hungry baby birds with a huge appetite.

一條多汁的大肥蟲就只能餵一小口，
填一填飢餓的鳥寶寶的大胃口。

yī tiáo duō zhī dī dà féi chóng jiù zhǐ wèi yī xiǎo kǒu
一条多汁的大肥虫就只喂一小口，
tián yī tián jī è dī niǎo bǎo bǎo dī dà wèi kǒu
填一填饥饿的鸟宝宝的大胃口。

The Life and Times of Baby Robins

Mother grabs as much food
as her bill will hold,
Then feeds her babies and
protects them from the cold.

鳥媽媽用鳥嘴儘量拿食物，
然後喂飽鳥寶寶也保護它們不會受凍。

niǎo mā ma yòng niǎo zuǐ jìn liáng ná shí wù
鸟妈妈用鸟嘴尽量拿食物，
rán hòu wèi bǎo niǎo bǎo bao yě bǎo hù tā men bù huì shòu dòng
然后喂饱鸟宝宝也保护它们不会受冻

The Life and Times of Baby Robins

Then the babies' feathers begin to grow;
Mother must work harder than
they'll ever know.

然後鳥寶寶的羽毛開始生長；
它們永遠不會知道鳥媽媽必須更加繁忙。

rán hòu niǎo bǎo bǎo di yǔ máo kāi shǐ shēng cháng
然后鸟宝宝的羽毛开始生长；
tā men yǒng yuǎn bù huì zhī dào niǎo mā mā bì xū gēng jiā fán máng
它们永远不会知道鸟妈妈必须更加繁忙。

The Life and Times of Baby Robins

The babies' wingspans begin to expand,
And mother bird will soon surely demand.

寶ㄅㄠˇ寶ㄅㄠˇ的ㄉㄜ˙翅ㄔˋ膀ㄅㄤˇ幅ㄈㄨˊ度ㄉㄨˋ開ㄎㄞ始ㄕˇ伸ㄕㄣ展ㄓㄢˇ,

鳥ㄋㄧㄠˇ媽ㄇㄚ媽ㄇㄚ不ㄅㄨˋ久ㄐㄧㄡˇ一ㄧ定ㄉㄧㄥˋ會ㄏㄨㄟˋ要ㄧㄠˋ看ㄎㄢˋ一ㄧ看ㄎㄢˋ。

bǎo bǎo de chì bǎng fú dù kāi shǐ shēn zhǎn
宝宝的翅膀幅度开始伸展,
niǎo mā mā bù jiǔ yī dìng huì yào kàn yī kàn
鸟妈妈不久一定会要看一看。

That these baby birds must now learn to fly;
It won't be long before they wave good-bye.

這些鳥寶寶們必須現在學會飛翔;
它們會不久就說再見, 揮揮翅膀。

这些鸟宝宝们必须现在学会飞翔,
它们会不久就说再见, 挥挥翅膀。

The Life and Times of Baby Robins

Flying a short distance to close twigs
and branches,
Baby birds are soon making big advances.

飛短距離到附近的小樹枝和大樹桿上，
鳥寶寶很快地進步向上。

飞短距离到附近的小树枝和大树杆上，
鸟宝宝很快地进步向上。

The Life and Times of Baby Robins

A few more days of worms, bugs, and seeds,
Will take good care of these
growing birds' needs.

再吃幾天蚯蚓、小蟲、和種子，
就可以好好照顧到成長中小鳥的需要。

再吃几天软虫、小虫、和种子，
就可以好好照顾到成长中小鸟的需要。

The Life and Times of Baby Robins

Now adults, the young birds wave
a cheerful good-bye;
Mother Robin says farewell with
a chirping sigh.

現在長大了， 它們搖搖翅膀開心地說見；
知更鳥媽媽啾啾地歎口氣說：
"珍重再見。"

现在长大了，它们摇摇翅膀开心地说再见；
知更鸟妈妈啾啾地叹口气说：
"珍重再见。"

Interesting Facts about Robins for Children

1. A robin is a well-known North American *thrush* (songbird) that grows about 9-19 inches (23-25 centimeters) long.
2. The male has an orange-red breast, brownish gray upper parts, and a blackish head.
3. The female bird is usually slightly smaller than the male and of *duller* color.
4. Robins are the state birds of Connecticut, Michigan, and Wisconsin.
5. Robins live in North America from Georgia to Alaska.
6. In winter, they may fly as far south as Mexico.
7. Robins are among the last birds to leave northern areas in autumn.
8. Often they *linger* until November, and sometimes they *remain* through the winter.
9. Robins are among the first birds to return north in spring. The first spring robin is a *popular sign* that winter will soon be over.
10. Robins are friendly and *gay*. They like to live in open areas near people.
11. Few birds have more beauty or a lovelier song than robins.
12. During the mating season, the males fill the air with joyful, ringing notes.
13. Their songs sound as if they were singing "cheerfully, cheerfully, and cheerfully."
14. Robins *frequently* return to the same place each year to build their nests.
15. Their favorite nesting places are in the fork between two braches on a *horizontal* branch, or on a shelf or *ledge* of a barn or house.
16. The nests form a cup-shaped *structure* from grass stems, roots, twigs, rags, strings, and paper. They use mud to hold the nest together. Then they lined it with dry grasses.
17. The females do most of the work of building the nest.
18. The females lay and *incubate* three to six delicate blue eggs for about two weeks.
19. When the young hatch, the male helps feed them.
20. Robins may have two or three *broods* during the spring and summer.

21. Robins are greedy eaters, and half of their diet *consists* of fruit They *prefer* wild fruit, and farmers can help protect crops by planting fruit-bearing trees nearby.

22. Robins also eat insects. They probably cause some harm because they catch useful earthworms.

23. Cats, snakes, and hawks prey upon the adult robin.

24. Squirrels, snakes, and other birds prey upon their eggs.

25. American robins are *common* in gardens, parks, yards, golf courses, fields, *pastures*, *tundra*, pine forests, woodlands, and forests.

26. The European robin is also called the *redbreast*, but they are about half the size of the American robins.

27. All robins are songbirds.

給小朋友
有關知更鳥的有趣知識

1. 知更鳥是北美洲大家知道的善鳴鳥（唱歌鳥），它大約有9-19寸（23-25公分）長。

2. 公鳥有橘紅色的胸脯棕灰色的上身，和黑色的頭。

3. 母鳥比公鳥小，顏色也黯淡些。

4. 知更鳥是肯納迪克州，密西根州，及威斯康欣州的州鳥。

5. 知更鳥住在北美洲，從喬治亞州到阿拉斯加州。

6. 冬天，它們向南遠飛到墨西哥。

7. 知更鳥是在秋天最後離開北方地區的鳥兒之一。

8. 它們停留到十一月。有時冬天也留下來。

9. 知更鳥是春天最早飛回北方的鳥兒。初春的知更鳥是人們知道冬天馬上要過去的訊號。

10. 知更鳥是友善和快樂的鳥。它們喜歡住在空曠近人的地方。

11. 很少鳥兒比知更鳥外表更美麗，歌聲更動人。

12. 在求偶的季節，公鳥把空中充滿快樂歡欣的歌聲。

13. 它們的歌聲好像在唱，"快樂，快樂，快樂。"

14. 知更鳥常常每年回到同樣的地方築巢。

15. 它們最喜歡築巢的地方就是橫的樹杆上，樹枝的分叉或是在架子上，或是房子穀倉的屋沿下。

16. 鳥巢是杯子形狀，用草梗、植物根、小枝、破布、線條、和紙做的。然後知更鳥把鳥巢墊上乾草。

17. 母鳥做大部分的築巢工作。

18. 母鳥生3-6個脆弱的藍色的小蛋，她孵蛋大約2個星期。

19. 小鳥孵出後，公鳥也幫忙餵小鳥。

20. 知更鳥春天和夏天可以生2-3窩小鳥。

21. 知更鳥胃口很大，它們的食物大半都是水果。它們喜歡野生水果。農夫可以在附近種些果樹來保護農作物。

22. 知更鳥也吃蟲子。它們可能造成些傷害，因為他們吃益蟲蚯蚓。

23. 貓、蛇、和鷹捕食知更鳥。

24. 松鼠、蛇、和其他的鳥吃知更鳥的蛋。

25. 美國知更鳥常在公園、庭院、高爾球場、田園、草原、凍土地帶、松林、林地、森林出現。

26. 歐洲知更鳥也叫做"紅胸脯"．但是它們只有美洲知更鳥一半大。

27. 所有的知更鳥都是善鳴鳥。

给小朋友
有关知更鸟的有趣知识

1. 知更鸟是北美洲大家知道的善鸣鸟（唱歌鸟），它大约有9-19寸（23-25公分）长。
2. 公鸟有橘红色的胸脯棕灰色的上身，和黑色的头。
3. 母鸟比公鸟小，颜色也黯淡些。
4. 知更鸟是肯纳迪克州，密西根州，及威斯康欣州的州鸟。
5. 知更鸟住在北美洲，从乔治亚州到阿拉斯加州。
6. 冬天，它们向南远飞到墨西哥。
7. 知更鸟是在秋天最后离开北方地区的鸟儿之一。
8. 它们停留到十一月。有时冬天也留下来。
9. 知更鸟是春天最早飞回北方的鸟儿。初春的知更鸟是人们知道冬天马上要过去的讯号。
10. 知更鸟是友善和快乐的鸟。它们喜欢住在空旷近人的地方。
11. 很少鸟儿比知更鸟外表更美丽歌声更动人。
12. 在求偶的季节，公鸟把空中充满快乐欢欣的歌声。
13. 它们的歌声好像在唱，"快乐，快乐，快乐。"
14. 知更鸟常常每年回到同样的地方筑巢。
15. 它们最喜欢筑巢的地方就是横的树杆上树枝的分叉，或是在架子上，或是房子谷仓的屋沿下。
16. 鸟巢是杯子形状，用草梗、植物根、小枝、破布、线条、和纸做的。然后知更鸟把鸟巢垫上干草。
17. 母鸟做大部分的筑巢工作。
18. 母鸟生3-6个脆弱的蓝色的小蛋，她孵蛋大约2个星期。

19. 小鸟孵出后，公鸟也帮忙喂小鸟。
20. 知更鸟春天和夏天可以生 2-3 窝小鸟。
21. 知更鸟胃口很大，它们的食物大半都是水果。它们喜欢野生水果。农夫可以在附近种些果树来保护农作物。
22. 知更鸟也吃虫子。它们可能造成些伤害，因为他们吃益虫蚯蚓。
23. 猫、蛇、和鹰捕食知更鸟。
24. 松鼠、蛇、和其他的鸟吃知更鸟的蛋。
25. 美国知更鸟常在公园、庭院、高尔球场、田园、草原、冻土地带、松林、林地、森林出现。
26. 欧洲知更鸟也叫做"红胸脯"．但是它们只有美洲知更鸟一半大。
27. 所有的知更鸟都是善鸣鸟。

Robins' Workshop for Children

1. Look at the pictures in the book and tell your family about robins.
2. Color the robin picture.
3. Go online to "Google" search for images and photographs of robins. Would you be interested in drawing a picture of a robin, or a nest with 3-6 blue eggs, or draw a few baby robins?
4. Build or buy a bird feed for your garden. Watch birds come and enjoy the treat.
5. Observe and find out what kind of birds come to your yard to visit you. For example, I always have small *humming birds* come to gather *nectar* of the *various* flowers in my front and back yards. I also find bigger birds come to share my peaches, grapes, and guavas.
6. Mrs. Shaw has crows that *disturb* her sleep in the morning. They all come in a huge group, sharing food and taking a bath in water *puddles*. There is always a *sentry* standing on the roof all day long, calling the others to come if there is food to share.
7. When you go to a park or outdoors with your family, what kind of birds do you see?

給小朋友
知更鳥工作室

1. 看看書裏的知更鳥圖畫。 告訴你的家人有關知更鳥的知識。

2. 把知更鳥的圖畫塗上顏色。

3. 上Google網站， 找一找 知更鳥的圖畫。 你要不要畫一張知更鳥的圖畫， 或是一個鳥窩有3-6個藍色的蛋， 或是畫幾隻知更鳥寶寶？

4. 買一個或建造一個餵鳥的小盒。 觀察鳥兒們來享受美味的鳥食。

5. 仔細觀察有什麼鳥兒來到你家來拜訪你。 我的家前後院有很多小蜂鳥來採不同花朵的花蜜。 我也看到大些的鳥來分享我家的桃子、 葡萄、 和番石榴。

6. 蕭婆婆 Mrs. Shaw 家有烏鴉早上打擾她的睡眠。 烏鴉都是一大群來分享食物在和水潭裏洗澡。 整天總是有一名哨兵烏鴉站在屋頂上， 假如有好吃的東西， 它就會叫其他的烏鴉來一同吃。

7. 當你和家人去公園戶外的時候， 你看到了什麼飛鳥？

给小朋友
知更鸟工作室

1. 看看书里的知更鸟图画。告诉你的家人有关知更鸟的知识。
2. 把知更鸟的图画涂上颜色。
3. 上 Google 网站，找一找 知更鸟的图画。你要不要画一张知更鸟的图画，或是一个鸟窝有 3-6 个蓝色的蛋，或是画几只知更鸟宝宝？
4. 买一个或建造一个喂鸟的小盒。观察鸟儿们来享受美味的鸟食。
5. 观察细看有什么鸟儿来到你家来拜访你。我的家前后院有很多小蜂鸟来采不同花朵的花蜜。我也看到大些的鸟来分享我家的桃子、葡萄、和番石榴。
6. Mrs. Shaw 萧婆婆家有乌鸦早上打扰她的睡眠。乌鸦都是一大群来分享食物在和水潭里洗澡。整天，总是有一名哨兵乌鸦站在屋顶上，假如有好吃的东西，它就会叫其他的乌鸦来一同吃。
7. 当你和家人去公园户外的时候，你看到了什么飞鸟？

Bird and Worm

鳥和蟲 鸟和虫
Niǎo Hé Chóng

Puppies, Puppies, Puppies

小ㄒㄧㄠˇ狗ㄍㄡˇ，小ㄒㄧㄠˇ狗ㄍㄡˇ，小ㄒㄧㄠˇ狗ㄍㄡˇ

xiǎo gǒu xiǎo gǒu xiǎo gǒu
小狗，小狗，小狗

Mildred Shaw & Dr. Loretta Huang 杜英慈 (dù yīng cí)

Illustrated by Abby Zhao 赵佳琦 (zhào jiā qí)

Puppies, Puppies, Puppies

小狗、小狗、小狗
xiǎo gǒu xiǎo gǒu xiǎo gǒu
小狗、小狗、小狗

We have been brought to the local pet store;
Mother dog could not keep us anymore.
We have grown and couldn't all fit in our bed.
More people with homes are needed we said.

We puppies are cute, neat, and clean,
And we are never, never mean.
We have got to learn quickly how to bark,
So we will practice as soon as its dark.
After breakfast we will practice some more;
Then look on people to come
through the door.
We wiggle our tongue and perk up our ears
And even our little bark we could hear.
We put out our tiny paws for little
handshakes;
We try to attract everyone
for goodness sake.

A man with his daughter and son
are first in line.
"Oh! My goodness," they say.
"We are just right in time."
"There are three puppies, and
there're three of us!"
"Buying three puppies is simply a must!"
Father says, "We have a yard and no other pet,
So we will all enjoy these puppies
you can bet."
So many tricks we'll learn to do,
But you must take us home with you.
We are lucky the Puppies say,
And we need names and each a bed.
We wonder what our names will be,
But will just have to wait and see.

Words of wisdom:

Correct practice makes perfect.

智慧之語：熟能生巧
zhì huì zhī yǔ   shú néng shēng qiǎo
智慧之语：熟能生巧

Puppies, Puppies, Puppies

We have been brought to the local pet store;
Mother dog could not keep us anymore.

小狗, 小狗, 小狗

我們被帶到當地的寵物店裏；
因為狗媽媽不能再留我們在家裏。

xiǎo gǒu　xiǎo gǒu　xiǎo gǒu
小狗，小狗，小狗

wǒ men bèi dài dào dāng dì dì chǒng wù diàn lǐ
我们被带到当地的宠物店里；
yīn wéi gǒu mā mā bù néng zài liú wǒ men zài jiā lǐ
因为狗妈妈不能再留我们在家里。

We have grown and couldn't all fit in our bed.
More people with homes are needed we said.

我們已經長大得床都裝不下了。
我們需要更多有家的人收養我們了。

wǒ men yǐ jīng cháng dà dé chuáng dū zhuāng bù xià liǎo
我们已经长大得床都装不下了。
wǒ men xū yào gēng duō yǒu jiā dì rén shōu yǎng wǒ men liǎo
我们需要更多有家的人收养我们了。

Puppies, Puppies, Puppies

We puppies are cute, neat, and clean,
And we are never, never mean.

我們小狗又可愛聰敏又乾淨整潔，
我們又從來不惡劣。

wǒ men xiǎo gǒu yòu kě ài cōng mǐn yòu qián jìng zhěng jié
我们小狗又可爱聪敏又乾净整洁，
wǒ men yòu cóng lái bù è liè
我们又从来不恶劣。

We have got to learn quickly how to bark,
So we will practice as soon as it's dark.

我們得很快學會狗叫，
所以天一黑我們就練習汪汪叫。

wǒ men dé hěn kuài xué huì gǒu jiào
我们得很快学会狗叫，
suǒ yǐ tiān yī hēi wǒ men jiù liàn xí wāng wāng jiào
所以天一黑我们就练习汪汪叫。

After breakfast we will practice some more;
Then look on people to come
through the door.

吃完早飯我們再多練習一會兒；
然後我們就看著進門來的人們。

chī wán zǎo fàn wǒ men zài duō liàn xí yī huì ér
吃完早饭我们再多练习一会儿；
rán hòu wǒ men jiù kàn zhù jìn mén lái dì rén men
然后我们就看著进门来的人们

Puppies, Puppies, Puppies

We wiggle our tongue and perk up our ears
And even our little bark we could hear.

我們搖動舌頭豎起耳朵

我們甚至能聽到我們輕輕的叫聲噢。

wǒ men yáo dòng shé tóu shù qǐ ěr duǒ
我们摇动舌头竖起耳朵
wǒ men shèn zhì néng tīng dào wǒ men qīng qīng dì jiào shēng ō
我们甚至能听到我们轻轻的叫声噢。

We put out our tiny paws
for little handshakes;
We try to attract everyone
for goodness sake.

我們把小爪子伸出去握握小手；
我們務必要引起每一個人的興趣噢。

我们把小爪子伸出去握握小手；
我们务必要引起每一个人的兴趣噢。

Puppies, Puppies, Puppies

A man with his daughter
and son are first in line.
"Oh! My goodness," they say.
"We are just right in time."

一個男人帶著他的女兒和兒子是
第一個排隊進來的人。
"啊哈！"他們說，"我們來得正是時辰。"

yī gè nán rén dài zhù tā dí nǚ ér hé ér zǐ shì dì yī gè
一个男人带著他的女儿和儿子是第一个
pái duì jìn lái dí rén
排队进来的人。
ā hā   tā men shuō   wǒ men lái dé zhèng shì shí chén
"啊哈！"他们说，"我们来得正是时辰。"

Puppies, Puppies, Puppies

"There are three puppies, and there're three of us!"
"Buying three puppies is simply a must!"

" 這兒有三隻小狗， 我們有三個人！ "
" 我們必須買三隻平分！ "

"zhè ér yǒu sān zhī xiǎo gǒu   wǒ men yǒu sān gè rén
这儿有三只小狗， 我们有三个人！ "
"wǒ men bì xū mǎi sān zhī píng fēn
我们必须买三只平分！ "

Puppies, Puppies, Puppies

Father says,
"We have a yard and no other pet,
So we will all enjoy these puppies
you can bet."

爸爸說，"我們有院子，而沒有其他的寵物，
所以，你們肯定會喜歡小狗的
樂趣和好處。"

bà bà shuō, "wǒ men yǒu yuàn zǐ, ér méi yǒu qí tā dì chǒng wù
爸爸说，"我们有院子，而没有其他的宠物，
suǒ yǐ, nǐ men kěn dìng huì xǐ huān xiǎo gǒu dì lè qù hé hǎo chù
所以，你们肯定会喜欢小狗的乐趣和好处。"

Puppies, Puppies, Puppies

So many tricks we'll learn to do,
But you must take us home with you.

我們會學做很多把戲,
但是你們必須帶我們回家去。

wǒ men huì xué zuò hěn duō bǎ xì
我们会学做很多把戏,
dàn shì nǐ men bì xū dài wǒ men huí jiā qù
但是你们必须带我们回家去。

Puppies, Puppies, Puppies

We are lucky the Puppies say,
And we need names and each a bed.

小狗說，" 我們好幸運幸福，我們每隻都要一個名字和一張床鋪。

xiǎo gǒu shuō， wǒ men hǎo xìng yùn xìng fú
小狗说，"我们好幸运幸福，
wǒ men měi zhī dū yào yī gè míng zì hé yī zhāng chuáng pū
我们每只都要一个名字和一张床铺。

Puppies, Puppies, Puppies

We wonder what our names will be,
But will just have to wait and see.

我們好奇我們的名字會是什麼呢，
但是只有等一會兒才會知道呢。"

我们好奇我们的名字会是什么呢，
但是只有等一会儿才会知道呢。"

Interesting Information about Puppies and Dogs for Children

Puppies

1. Puppy is what we call very young dogs.

2. A mother (*female*) dog *carries* her young for nine weeks before puppies are born.

3. In most cases, a dog gives birth to a *litter* of 1 to 12 puppies.

4. A mother dog *nurses* her puppies on milk *produced* by her body until her pups are about 6 weeks old.

5. Puppies are born with their eyes closed and their ears *sealed*. Their eyes and ears open about 13 to 15 days after birth.

6. Puppies begin to walk and to respond to sights and sounds during their (a) second week (b) **third week** (c) fourth week of life.

7. Between 4 and 10 weeks of age, a puppy forms emotional attachments to its mother, its *littermates*, and people.

8. If the puppy is to become a good pet, it must have contact with people during this period to develop a *close relationship* that will last *throughout* its life. For this reason, the *ideal* time to adopt a puppy is 6 to 8 weeks old.

9. Dogs become fully grown at 8 months to 2 years of age *depending* on the size of the *breed*.

10. A 2-year-old dog compares to a (a) 12- year-old (b) 20-year-old (c) **24-years** old person.

11. On the *average*, dogs live about (a) 8 to 11 years (b) **12 to 15 years** (c) 16 to 19 years.

12. By the age of 4 weeks, a puppy can produce a full range of *vocal* sounds—barks, growls, howls, whines, and yelps. Some of these sounds have different *meanings* in different *situations*.

13. Puppies also use body language to *communicate* their feelings and desires.

14. The puppies' body language may be (a) **pawing** (b) **wagging the tail** (c) **showing eye contact**
15. Be on guard if a dog *stiffens* up, holds its tail high, snarls, and stares at you.
16. Puppies should be fed small *amounts* (a) two times (b) three times (c) **four times a day.**

Dogs

17. Dog is a *popular* pet (a) in America (b) in China (c) **throughout the world.**
18. At least 12,000 years ago, dogs became the first animals to be *tamed*.
19. Through careful *breeding*, humans have produced hundreds of breeds.
20. The smallest *breed* is the (a) poodle (b) **Chihuahua** (c) Cocker Spaniel.
21. The heaviest dog is St Bernard.
22. Dogs belong to the same family as foxes, wolves, *coyotes*, and *jackals*.
23. Most dogs have two coats—the outer coat to *protect* the dog against rain and snow, the under coat to keep the dog warm.
24. All dogs have the same number of bones 321 in total, but the size and shape of the bones differ greatly from *breed* to *breed*.
25. Dogs have four toes on each foot plus an extra thumb-like toe on each front foot.
26. Dogs, like cats, can pull their *claws* back. (a) True (b) **False**
27. Puppies have 32 *temporary* teeth, which they begin to lose when they are about 5 months old. *Adult* doges have 42 teeth.
28. Many breeds of dogs have pointed ears that stand straight up. Other breeds have hanging-down ears.
29. A dog's *temperature* is a little higher that a person's normal *temperature* of 98.6 °F (or 37°C).
30. Dogs do not cool the body by *sweating* like humans. Instead, a dog sticks out its tongue and pants.
31. A dog's most highly developed sense is smell. Dogs can *detect* some odors that are *millions* of times too *faint* for people to *detect*.
32. *Fluid* from a *gland* inside the nose keeps the tip of a dog's nose *moist*. The *moisture* helps a dog *detect* odors.

33. A dog also licks its nose to help it *moist*.

34. A dog's *whiskers* may sense the wind *directions* from which an odor is coming.

35. Dogs have much better sense of hearing than people have. Dogs can hear *higher-pitched* sounds and sounds from much *greater distances* than people can.

36. Dogs can see as well as people. (a)True (b) **False**.

37. Dogs detect *movement* better than people.

38. Dogs are *color blind*. They can tell colors apart only by *recognizing* various shades of gray.

39. Dogs will *groom* each other and enjoy being *stroked* and petted by people.

40. Dogs that have been mistreated may show "*touch-shyness*" and avoid any *human contact*.

41. Most adult dogs *require* only one meal a day

42. Many dogs do *important* work for people because they are *intelligent* and *devoted* to their owners.

43. Different dogs can (a) **protect** houses and **businesses** from **burglars** (b) **herd live stock** (c) **help farmers by** *hauling produce* to market (d) *transport* people (e) *race*.

44. Dogs use their keen senses to (a) **track wild animals in** *hunting* (b) **help police sniff** out *illegal* **drugs and hidden** *explosives* (c) **lead** *blind* or *deaf people*.

45. Dogs are used in *medical* treatment and in *research*.

給小朋友
有關小狗和狗的有趣常識
小狗

1. 小狗是很年輕的狗。

2. 狗媽媽（母狗）懷孕九個星期才生下小狗。

3. 大多時候，狗一次生 1-12 隻小狗。

4. 母狗用她身體產生的奶喂小狗到 6 周（星期）大。

5. 小狗出生的時候，它們的眼睛閉著，耳朵關著。它們的眼睛和耳朵在出生後 13-15 天才打開。

6. 小狗開始行走、對影像和聲音有反應是在它們生下（a）第二 （b）第三 （c）第四 周的時候。

7. 在 4-10 周大的時候，小狗開始和它的媽媽、同一窩的小狗、和人養成感情的聯繫。

8. 如果想把小狗養成好寵物，它必須在這個時候和人們培養持續一生的親蜜關係。所以，領養小狗最理想的時候是 6-8 周。

9. 不同的品種和大小的狗，在 8 個月到 2 年就長成了。

10. 兩（2）歲的狗等于（a）12 歲 （b）20 歲 （c）24 歲的人類。

11. 一般來說，狗大約活（a）8-11 年 （b）12-15 年 （c）16-19 年。

12. 小狗大約 4 周大的時候，可以叫出全部的聲音 --- 大聲吠叫、低沈怒吼、哀聲嚎叫、嗚嗚悲鳴、痛苦或興奮地叫喚。這些聲音在不同的情況有不同的意思。

13. 小狗也用身體語言來表達它的感覺和欲望。

14. 小狗的身體語言可能是（a）用爪子抓你（b）搖尾巴（c）用眼睛看著你。

15. 假如狗的身體僵直、尾巴高舉、厲聲咆哮、還兩眼直瞪著你，你必須要小心！

16. 小狗應該餵少量食物，一天四（4）次。

狗

17. 狗是一個在（a）美國（b）中國（c）世界上很受歡迎的寵物。

18. 至少在 12,000 年以前，狗已經是最先被馴服的動物。

19. 仔細地配種，人類已經培養出幾百種狗的品種。

20. 最小的狗品種是（a）poodle 有卷曲厚毛的狗（b）Chihuahua 奇娃娃狗（c）Cocker Spaniel 長毛垂耳的狗。

21. 最重的狗是 Saint Bernard 雪地救人狗。

22. 狗和狐狸、野狼、郊狼、胡狼都是同一個類的動物。

23. 多數的狗有兩層皮毛——外層保護狗不怕雨雪，下層的毛皮保暖。

24. 所有的狗都有同樣數目的骨頭一共 321 塊，但是骨頭的大小和型狀每個品種都不同。

25. 狗每隻腳有四個趾頭，在每隻前腳也有一個像的姆指一樣的腳趾。

26. 狗像貓一樣，能把尖爪子收縮起來。 不對

27. 小狗有 32 顆臨時的乳齒，在 5 個月大的時候開始掉下。長成的狗有 42 顆牙齒。

28. 很多品種的狗有豎起來的尖耳朵。其他品種有垂下來的耳朵。

29. 狗的體溫比人的正常體溫 98.6°F（或 37°C）略為高些。

30. 狗不像人用流汗來降低體溫。它們伸出舌頭喘氣來降低體溫。

31. 狗最發達的感官是嗅覺。狗可以察覺一些氣味，幾百萬倍人們察覺不到的氣味。

32. 狗鼻子裏的腺體，流出液體保持狗鼻子潮濕。這潮濕的鼻子幫助狗查覺氣味。

33. 狗也舔鼻子讓鼻子潮濕。

34. 狗的鬍鬚能感覺風的方向，知道氣味從那個方向來。

35. 狗的聽覺比人好。狗可以聽見高頻率的聲音，和比人能聽到的距離更遠。

36. 狗能看得和人一樣清楚。不對

37. 狗比人更能察覺移動活動。

38. 狗有色盲。它們用不同深淺的灰色來分辨顏色。

39. 狗會彼此修飾整潔，也喜愛人們摸它拍它。

40. 被虐待的狗會"害羞人摸它"，也會避免和人接觸。

41. 大部分的成年狗只需要一天餵一次。

42. 很多狗為人們做重要的工作，因為它們又聰明，對主人又忠心。

43. 不同的狗能 (a) 保護房屋及商店不受小偷光顧 (b) 看顧牛羊群 (c) 幫助農夫把蔬果拉到市場 (d) 拉車做交通工具 (e) 賽狗/賽狗車。

44. 狗用它敏銳的感官 (a) 在打獵時追尋獵物 (b) 幫助警察聞出非法毒品和爆炸物 (c) 領導盲眼或耳聾的人。

45. 狗也用在醫藥治療和醫藥研究上。

给小朋友
有关小狗和狗的有趣常识
小狗

1. 小狗是很年轻的狗。
2. 狗妈妈（母狗）怀孕九个星期才生下小狗。
3. 大多时候，狗一次生 1-12 只小狗。
4. 母狗用她身体产生的奶喂小狗到 6 周（星期）大。
5. 小狗出生的时候，它们的眼睛闭着，耳朵关着。它们的眼睛和耳朵在出生后 13-15 天才打开。
6. 小狗开始行走、对影像和声音有反应是在它们生下 (a) 第二 (b) 第三 (c) 第四周的时候。
7. 在 4-10 周大的时候，小狗开始和它的妈妈、同一窝的小狗、和人养成感情的联系。
8. 如果想把小狗养成好宠物，它必须在这个时候和人们培养持续一生的亲蜜关系。所以，领养小狗最理想的时候是 6-8 周。
9. 不同的品种和大小的狗，在 8 个月到 2 年就长成了。

10. 两（2）岁的狗等于（a）12 岁（b）20 岁（c）**24 岁的人类**。

11. 一般来说，狗大约活（a）8-11 年（b）**12-15 年**（c）16-19 年。

12. 小狗大约4周大的时候，可以叫出全部的声音——大声吠叫、低沉怒吼、哀声嚎叫、呜呜悲鸣、痛苦或兴奋地叫嚷。这些声音在不同的情况有不同的意思。

13. 小狗也用身体语言来表达它的感觉和欲望。

14. 小狗的身体语言可能是（a）**用爪子抓你**（b）**摇尾巴**（c）**用眼睛看着你**。

15. 假如狗的身体僵直、尾巴高举、厉声咆哮、还两眼直瞪着你，你必须要小心！

16. 小狗应该喂少量食物，**一天四（4）次**。

狗

17. 狗是一个在（a）美国（b）中国（c）**世界上**很受欢迎的宠物。

18. 至少在 12,000 年以前，狗已经是最先被驯服的动物。

19. 仔细地配种，人类已经培养出几百种狗的品种。

20. 最小的狗品种是（a）poodle 有卷曲厚毛的狗（b）**Chihuahua 奇娃娃狗**（c）Cocker Spaniel 长毛垂耳的狗。

21. 最重的狗是 Saint Bernard 雪地救人狗。

22. 狗和狐狸、野狼、郊狼、胡狼都是同一个类的动物。

23. 多数的狗有两层皮毛—外层保护狗不怕雨雪，下层的毛皮保暖。

24. 所有的狗都有同样数目的骨头一共321块，但是骨头的大小和型状，每个品种都不同。

25. 狗每只脚有四个趾头，在每只前脚也有一个像的姆指一样的脚趾。

26. 狗像猫一样，能把尖爪子收缩起来。**不对**

27. 小狗有32颗临时的乳齿,在5个月大的时候开始掉下。长成的狗有42颗牙齿。

28. 很多品种的狗有竖起来的尖耳朵。其他品种有垂下来的耳朵。

29. 狗的体温比人的正常体温98.6℉（或37℃）略为高些。

30. 狗不像人用流汗来降低体温。它们伸出舌头喘气来降低体温。

31. 狗最发达的感官是嗅觉。狗可以察觉一些气味,几百万倍人们察觉不到的气味。

32. 狗鼻子里的腺体,流出液体保持狗鼻子潮湿。这潮湿的鼻子帮助狗查觉气味。

33. 狗也舔鼻子让鼻子潮湿。

34. 狗的胡须能感觉风的方向,知道气味从那个方向来。

35. 狗的听觉比人好。狗可以听见高频率的声音,和比人能听到的距离更远。

36. 狗能看得和人一样清楚。不对

37. 狗比人更能察觉移动活动。

38. 狗有色盲。它们用不同深浅的灰色来分辨颜色。

39. 狗会彼此修饰整洁,也喜爱人们摸它拍它。

40. 被虐待的狗会"害羞人摸它",也会避免和人接触。

41. 大部分的成年狗只需要一天喂一次。

42. 很多狗为人们做重要的工作,因为它们又聪明,对主人又忠心。

43. 不同的狗能（a）保护房屋及商店不受小偷光顾（b）看顾牛羊群（c）帮助农夫把蔬果拉到市场（d）拉车做交通工具（e）赛狗/赛狗车。

44. 狗用它敏锐的感官（a）在打猎时追寻猎物（b）帮助警察闻出非法毒品和爆炸物（c）领导盲眼或耳聋的人。

45. 狗也用在医药治疗和医药研究上。

Puppies & Dogs Workshop for Children

1. Collect pictures of puppies or dogs. Describe them to your family.
2. Visit a pet store and observe the behavior of the puppies. Share your findings with your family or friends.
3. Draw a picture of a puppy or a dog that you would like to keep in your scrapbook.
4. Would you like to adopt a puppy as a pet? Why or why not?
5. If you would like to adopt a puppy into your family, how would your family prepare for it?

給小朋友
小狗工作室

1. 收集小狗或狗的圖片。給家人說明這些圖片。
2. 參觀一個寵物店，觀察小狗的行為。把你發現的事講給家人和好朋友聽。
3. 畫一隻小狗或大狗。把它收藏在你的收藏簿裏。
4. 你想要收養一隻小狗或一個寵物嗎？為什麼要，或不要？
5. 假如你家要收養一隻小狗，你和家人要如何準備呢？

给小朋友
小狗工作室

1. 收集小狗或狗的图片。给家人说明这些图片。
2. 参观一个宠物店,观察小狗的行为。把你发现的事讲给家人和好朋友听。
3. 画一只小狗或大狗。把它收藏在你的收藏簿里。
4. 你想要收养一只小狗或一个宠物吗?为什么要,或不要?
5. 假如你家要收养一只小狗,你和家人要如何准备呢?

Rabbit Eggs

兔ㄊㄨˋ子ㄗˇ蛋ㄉㄢˋ

_{tù zǐ dàn}
兔子蛋

Mildred Shaw & Dr. Loretta Huang 杜英慈 _{dù yīng cí}

Illustrated by Charles Chang 张以昕 _{zhāng yǐ xīn}

Rabbit Eggs

兔ㄊㄨˋ子ㄗˇ蛋ㄉㄢˋ

tù zǐ dàn
兔子蛋

Rabbits live in Rabbit Town;
Each den is safely underground.
We've lived here for so many years
With much work piled up to our ears.
Shelves in our dens are fully lined
With Easter Eggs of just one kind.
Into a mold with sugar'n cream
Eggs are shaped by each rabbit team.
We form our eggs to suit your taste;
No eggs we make will go to waste.
Marshmallow eggs are purely white;
Children eat them with true delight
Many eggs are red, white, or blue;
The eggs' color is up to you.
How's purple, orange, or yellow
On tasty eggs of marshmallow?
They may be chocolate. or cherry,
Or flavors of mango or strawberry.
In each den, there's just one color;
At night, we trade with each other.
We hide eggs nearly everywhere
To make hunting them always fair.
Easter morning children will dash,
Finding eggs hidden In the grass.
We rabbits work hard night and day,
So Easter we can hop and play.
At Enter time our eggs galore
Are sold in almost every store.

Some are big, others are tiny;
Children like them bright and shiny.
Eat only what one hand can pick
If you eat more, you may get sick.
Adults, also, enjoy these sweets
And think of them as Easter treats.
When our season's work is all done,
We all agree that we've had fun.
We'll to back to our home in the ground
For another year to come around.

Words of wisdom:

All work and no play make Jack a dull boy!

智慧之語：只工作（只讀書）不遊戲會養成遲鈍的孩子！

zhì huì zhī yǔ   zhǐ gōng zuò   zhǐ dú shū   bù yóu xì huì yǎng chéng chí dùn dì hái zǐ

智慧之语：只工作（只读书）不游戏会养成迟钝的孩子！

Rabbit Eggs

Rabbits live in Rabbit Town;
Each den is safely underground.

兔ㄊㄨˋ子ㄗ˙蛋ㄉㄢˋ

我ㄨㄛˇ們ㄇㄣ˙兔ㄊㄨˋ子ㄗ˙都ㄉㄡ住ㄓㄨˋ在ㄗㄞˋ兔ㄊㄨˋ子ㄗ˙鎮ㄓㄣˋ裏ㄌㄧˇ；
每ㄇㄟˇ一ㄧ個ㄍㄜˋ窩ㄨㄛ都ㄉㄡ是ㄕˋ安ㄢ全ㄑㄩㄢˊ地ㄉㄧˋ挖ㄨㄚ在ㄗㄞˋ地ㄉㄧˋ底ㄉㄧˇ。

tù zǐ dàn
兔子蛋

wǒ men tù zǐ dū zhù zài tù zǐ zhèn lǐ
我们兔子都住在兔子镇里；
měi yī gè wō dū shì ān quán dì wā zài dì dǐ
每一个窝都是安全地挖在地底。

Rabbit Eggs

We've lived here for so many years
With much work piled up to our ears.

我ㄨㄛˇ們ㄇㄣ˙已ㄧˇ經ㄐㄧㄥ在ㄗㄞˋ這ㄓㄜˋ兒ㄦ住ㄓㄨˋ了ㄌㄜ˙很ㄏㄣˇ多ㄉㄨㄛ年ㄋㄧㄢˊ了ㄌㄜ˙

很ㄏㄣˇ多ㄉㄨㄛ工ㄍㄨㄥ作ㄗㄨㄛˋ都ㄉㄡ堆ㄉㄨㄟ積ㄐㄧ到ㄉㄠˋ齊ㄑㄧˊ耳ㄦˇ朵ㄉㄨㄛ˙了ㄌㄜ˙。

wǒ men yǐ jīng zài zhè ér zhù liǎo hěn duō nián liǎo
我们已经在这儿住了很多年了
hěn duō gōng zuò dū duī jī dào qí ěr duǒ liǎo
很多工作都堆积到齐耳朵了。

Rabbit Eggs

Shelves in our dens are fully lined
With Easter Eggs of just one kind.

我們窩裏的架子排得滿滿
只有一種的復活節彩蛋。

wǒ men wō lǐ dì jià zǐ shàng pái dé mǎn mǎn
我们窝里的架子上排得满满
zhǐ yǒu yī zhǒng dì fù huó jié cǎi dàn
只有一种的复活节彩蛋。

Rabbit Eggs

Into a mold with sugar'n cream
Eggs are shaped by each rabbit team.

把白糖和奶油倒進模子裏

每一個兔子隊就把蛋完成了。

bǎ bái táng hé nǎi yóu dǎo jìn mó zǐ lǐ
把白糖和奶油倒进模子里
měi yī gè tù zǐ duì jiù bǎ dàn wán chéng liǎo
每一个兔子队就把蛋完成了。

Rabbit Eggs

We form our eggs to suit your taste;
No eggs we make will go to waste.

我們把蛋做成適合你的口味；
我們做的蛋沒有一個會浪費。

我们把蛋做成适合你的口味；
我们做的蛋没有一个会浪费。

Rabbit Eggs

Marshmallow eggs are purely white;
Children eat them with true delight

棉軟糖蛋是純白色；
孩子吃那種蛋真是太開心了。

mián ruǎn táng dàn shì chún bái sè
棉软糖蛋是纯白色；
hái zǐ chī nà zhǒng dàn zhēn shì tài kāi xīn liǎo
孩子吃那种蛋真是太开心了。

White Rabbit Eggs

Red Rabbit Eggs

Rabbit Eggs

Many eggs are red, white, or blue;
The eggs' colon an up to you.

許多蛋是紅色、白色、或藍色；
由你決定蛋的顏色。

xǔ duō dàn shì hóng sè　bái sè　huò lán sè
许多蛋是红色、白色、或蓝色；
yóu nǐ jué dìng dàn dí yán sè
由你决定蛋的颜色。

Rabbit Eggs

How's purple, orange, or yellow
On tasty eggs of marshmallow?

把紫色、橘色、或黃色
染在好吃的棉軟糖蛋上好不好？

bǎ zǐ sè、 jú sè、 huò huáng sè
把紫色、橘色、或黃色
rǎn zài hǎo chī dì mián ruǎn táng dàn shàng hǎo bù hǎo
染在好吃的棉软糖蛋上好不好？

Rabbit Eggs

They may be chocolate. or cherry,
Or flavors of mango or strawberry.

彩蛋可以是巧克力, 或櫻桃,
或者是芒果或莓子的味道。

cǎi dàn kě yǐ shì qiǎo kè lì, huò yīng táo,
彩蛋可以是巧克力, 或櫻桃,
huò zhě shì máng guǒ huò méi zǐ dí wèi dào
或者是芒果或莓子的味道。

Rabbit Eggs

In each den, there's just one color;
At night, we trade with each other.

每一個窩裏, 只有一種顏色的彩蛋;
晚上, 我們就出來交換。

每一个窝里,我们只有一种颜色的彩蛋;
晚上,我们就出来交换。

Rabbit Eggs

We hide eggs nearly everywhere
To make hunting them always fair.

我們把蛋藏在幾乎每一個地方
讓找蛋的遊戲總是公平順當。

wǒ men bǎ dàn cáng zài jǐ hū měi yī gè dì fāng
我们把蛋藏在几乎每一个地方
ràng zhǎo dàn dì yóu xì zǒng shì gōng píng shùn dāng
让找蛋的游戏总是公平顺当。

Rabbit Eggs

Easter morning children will dash,
Finding eggs hidden in the grass.

復活節早上孩子們會衝出去看,
尋找藏在草裏的彩蛋。

fù huó jié zǎo shàng hái zǐ men huì chōng chū qù kàn
复活节早上孩子们会忡出去看,
xún zhǎo cáng zài cǎo lǐ dì cǎi dàn
寻找藏在草里的彩蛋。

Rabbit Eggs

We rabbits work hard night and day,
So Easter we can hop and play.

我們兔子日夜工作，
在復活節我們才能又蹦跳又玩樂。

我们兔子日夜工作，
wǒ men tù zǐ rì yè gōng zuò

在复活节我们才能又蹦跳又玩乐。
zài fù huó jié wǒ men cái néng yòu bèng tiào yòu wán lè

Rabbit Eggs

At Enter time our eggs galore
Are sold in almost every store.

復活節時我們的糖蛋豐富多彩
幾乎在每一個店鋪都有得賣。

fù huó jié shí wǒ men di táng dàn fēng fù duō cǎi
复活节时我们的糖蛋丰富多彩
jī hū zài měi yī gè diàn pū dū yǒu dé mài
几乎在每一个店铺都有得卖。

Rabbit Eggs

Some are big, others are tiny;
Children like them bright and shiny.

彩蛋有大, 也有小；
小朋友們喜歡彩蛋明亮又光耀。

cǎi dàn yǒu dà, yě yǒu xiǎo
彩蛋有大, 也有小；
xiǎo péng yǒu men xǐ huān cǎi dàn míng liàng yòu guāng yào
小朋友们喜欢彩蛋明亮又光耀。

Rabbit Eggs

Eat only what one hand can pick;
If you eat more, you may get sick.

彩蛋你只能吃一隻能拿的幾個；
如果多吃，你就會生病了。

cǎi dàn nǐ zhǐ néng chī yī zhǐ shǒu néng ná dì jǐ gè
彩蛋你只能吃一只手能拿的几个；
rú guǒ duō chī nǐ jiù huì shēng bìng liǎo
如果多吃，你就会生病了。

Adults also enjoy these sweets
And consider them Easter treat.

大人也喜歡吃這些甜食
也認為彩蛋是復活節的樂事。

dà rén yě xǐ huān chī zhè xiē tián shí
大人也喜欢吃这些甜食
yě rèn wéi cǎi dàn shì fù huó jié dì lè shì
也认为彩蛋是复活节的乐事。

Rabbit Town Exit

Rabbit Eggs

When our season's work is all done,
We all agree that we've had fun.

當我們一個季節的工作都做完畢，
我們都同意我們工作得很有趣。

dāng wǒ men yī gè jì jié dí gōng zuò dū zuò wán bì
当我们一个季节的工作都做完毕，
wǒ men dū tóng yì wǒ men gōng zuò dé hěn yǒu qù
我们都同意我们工作得很有趣。

Rabbit Eggs

We'll to back to our home in the ground
For another year to come around.

我們都要回到我們地下的家

等待明年再來啊。

wǒ men dū yào huí dào wǒ men dì xià dì jiā
我们都要回到我们地下的家
děng dài míng nián zài lái ā
等待明年再来啊。

Interesting Rabbit Egg Information for Children

1. Easter in the United States is *celebrated* on a Sunday in spring.

2. In many areas in the United States, children collect candy and chocolate bunnies, and hunt colorful Easter eggs that *contains* small goodies.

3. Easter egg hunts are fun *activities* for both children and adults.

4. Eggs represent the new life in many *cultures*.

5. In general, *Christians* around the world *celebrate* Easter.

6. Many different countries *celebrate* Easter in different ways.

7. Easter eggs have become a *popular* part of Easter *celebration* in many countries.

8. On the Monday after Easter, the President of the United States welcomes thousands of children to the White House lawn in Washington D.C. for an egg-rolling contest.

9. Many people wear new spring clothes to church on Easter.

10. Rabbits walk or run as most four-legged animals do. (**False**)

11. A rabbit moves about by hopping on its longer and stronger *hind* Legs and *balancing* its body with the front legs.

12. When chased by an *enemy*, a rabbit on hop as fast as (a) 8 miles an hour (b) **18 miles an hour** (c) 28 miles an hotel (about 29 kilometers).

13. Most rabbits live in a *shallow* hole hidden in bushes, shaft, weeds, grasses or leaves.

14. Those of the northern United States and Canada may live in a *Burrow* under pile of *brush*, rocks, or wood. They move into the *burrows abandoned* by other animals.

15. Most rabbits spend the day eating, playing, resting, and sleeping.

16. Rabbits eat meat and candy as well as grains and plant food. (a)True (b) **False**

17. A *female* cottontail rabbit does not lay eggs. She carries her young inside her body for 26 to 30 days before bath.

18. A mother rabbit may have 2 to 9 *young kits(or kittens)* that cannot see or hear nor have any *fur* at birth.

19. Wild rabbits live long in *captivity.* (a) True (b) **False**

20. Rabbits are raised for their meat and fur, for use in *scientific* research, and as pets.

21. Most rabbits like to be held or petted often. (a) True (b) **False**

22. Never lift a rabbit by its ears or legs.

23. To lift a rabbit, we *grasp* the loose skin over the animal's *shoulders* with one hand, and place the other hand under the *rump* to support the rabbit's weight."

24. *Angora* rabbits are raised for their fur. The long hairs are *plucked* from the animals coats and *spun* into soft *yarn*.

給小朋友
有關兔子蛋的有趣常識

1. 美國是在春天裏的一個星期日過復活節。
2. 在美國很多地方的復活節，小朋友們收集糖果和巧克力兔子，也尋找彩色的蛋，裡面裝了小小的好東西。
3. 復活節找彩蛋是小朋友和大人都喜歡的活動。
4. 在許多國家和不同的文化，雞蛋代表新生命。
5. 一般來說，世界各地的基督徒會慶祝復活節。
6. 不同的國家有不同慶祝復活節的習俗。
7. 在很多國家，復活節彩蛋已經成為很流行的慶祝活動的一部分。
8. 復活節後的星期一，美國總統在首都華府白宮草坪上歡迎幾千個兒童舉行滾蛋比賽。
9. 在復活節，許多人穿新的春裝去教堂。
10. 兔子像多數四隻腳的動物一樣，又走又跑。（不是）
11. 兔子用長而有力的後腿跳動，用前腳平衡它的身體。
12. 當敵人追的時候，兔子每小時跳（8里，18里，28里，）（約29公里）。
13. 大部分的兔子住在密樹叢、矮灌木、野草、和樹葉遮蔽的淺洞裏。
14. 在美國北部和加拿大兔子住在矮樹叢、石頭、或木頭堆下面的地道裏。它們搬到其他動物丟棄的地道裏住。
15. 多數的兔子一天就吃、玩兒、休息、和睡覺。

16. 兔子吃肉和糖果，也吃穀類和植物。（不是）

17. 棉花尾巴的母兔子不生蛋。她在身體裏懷著小寶寶 26-30 天，才生下小兔子寶寶。

18. 兔子媽媽一次可以生 2-9 隻兔寶寶。兔寶寶生下來的時候看不見，聽不到，也沒有兔毛。

19. 野兔子被抓起來，可以活很久。（不是）

20. 人們飼養兔子是為了它的皮毛、肉、做科學實驗、和做小寵物。

21. 多數的兔子喜歡常常被抱著或撫摸。（不是）

22. 千萬不要抓著兔子的耳朵或腿把它提起來。

23. 抓兔子的時候，用一只手抓著它肩膀上的鬆皮，另一隻手托著兔子的臀部，把它提起來。

25. 人們為了毛飼養安哥拉兔子。兔子身上的長毛可以紡績成柔軟的毛線。

给小朋友
有关兔子蛋的有趣常识

1. 美国是在春天里的一个星期日过复活节。
2. 在美国很多地方的复活节,小朋友们收集糖果和巧克力兔子,也寻找彩色的蛋里面装了小小的好东西。
3. 复活节找彩蛋是小朋友和大人都喜欢的活动。
4. 在许多国家和不同的文化,鸡蛋代表新生命。
5. 一般来说,世界各地的基督徒会庆祝复活节。
6. 不同的国家有不同庆祝复活节的习俗。
7. 在很多国家,复活节彩蛋已经成为很流行的庆祝活动的一部分。
8. 复活节后的星期一,美国总统在首都华府白宫草坪上欢迎几千个儿童举行滚蛋比赛。
9. 在复活节,许多人穿新的春装去教堂。
10. 兔子像多数四只脚的动物一样,又走又跑。(不是)
11. 兔子用长而有力的后腿跳动,用前脚平衡它的身体。
12. 当敌人追的时候,兔子每小时跳(8里,18里,28里)(约29公里)。
13. 大部分的兔子住在密树茨、矮灌木、野草、和树叶遮蔽的浅洞里。
14. 在美国北部和加拿大兔子住在矮树茨、石头、或木头堆下面的地道里。它们搬到其他动物丢弃的地道里住。
15. 多数的兔子一天就吃、玩儿、休息、和睡觉。
16. 兔子吃肉和糖果,也吃谷类和植物。(不是)
17. 棉花尾巴的母兔子不生蛋。她在身体里怀着小宝宝26-30天,才生下小宝宝。

18. 兔子妈妈一次可以生2-9只兔宝宝。兔宝宝生下来的时候看不见，听不到，也没有兔毛。

19. 野兔子被抓起来，可以活很久。（不是）

20. 人们饲养兔子是为了它的皮毛、肉、做科学实验、和做小宠物。

21. 多数的兔子喜欢常常被抱着或抚摸。（不是）

22. 千万不要抓着兔子的耳朵或腿把它提起来。

23. 抓兔子的时候，用一只手抓着它肩膀上的松皮，另一只手托着兔子的臀部，把它提起来。

24. 人们为了毛饲养安哥拉兔子。兔子身上的长毛可以纺绩成柔软的毛线。

Rabbit Eggs Workshop for Children

Color Easter Eggs

Items: 6 eggs, 6 small bowls, soup spoons, water, salt, vinegar, food colors, tissue paper, and old newspaper

Optional items: stickers or crayons, rubber bands, old toothbrush.

How to Make and Color a Hard Boiled Egg:

1) Lay eggs on bottom of the pot. (Try not to stack eggs. It is better to do it in batches than overfill your pot.)
2) Fill with water so it is an inch over the eggs.
3) Put on high heat and bring to a rapid boil.
4) Let boil for 3 minutes. Turn off stove or remove pot from fire. Let eggs sit in hot water until water cools down. (about 12 minutes)
5) Remove the eggs from the pot and plunge them into cold water until you can pick them out of the water without burning your hands.
6) Spread old newspaper on table.
7) Put each food color, water, and vinegar in different bowls.
8) Put stickers on eggshells or use crayons to draw designs on eggshells.
9) Put eggs in small bowls with colored water. Let it soak for five (5) minutes. Dip eggs out with a spoon.
10) Dry eggs with tissue paper.
11) Eggs are colored!

To make other varieties of colored Easter eggs, see the following:
Food Coloring Dyed Easter Eggs

食ㄕ品ㄆㄧㄣ顏ㄧㄢ料ㄌㄧㄠ染ㄖㄢ復ㄈㄨ活ㄏㄨㄛ節ㄐㄧㄝ彩ㄘㄞ蛋ㄉㄢ

Tissue Paper Dyed Easter Eggs
衛ㄨㄟ生ㄕㄥ紙ㄓ復ㄈㄨ活ㄏㄨㄛ節ㄐㄧㄝ彩ㄘㄞ蛋ㄉㄢ

wèi shēng zhǐ fù huó jié cǎi dàn

卫生纸复活节彩蛋

Crayon Easter Eggs
蠟ㄌㄚ筆ㄅㄧ復ㄈㄨ活ㄏㄨㄛ節ㄐㄧㄝ彩ㄘㄞ蛋ㄉㄢ

là bǐ fù huó jié cǎi dàn

蜡笔复活节彩蛋

Sticker Easter Eggs
貼ㄊㄧㄝ紙ㄓ復ㄈㄨ活ㄏㄨㄛ節ㄐㄧㄝ彩ㄘㄞ蛋ㄉㄢ

tiē zhǐ fù huó jié cǎi dàn

贴纸复活节彩蛋

Marbleized Easter Eggs
大ㄉㄚ理ㄌㄧ石ㄕ復ㄈㄨ活ㄏㄨㄛ節ㄐㄧㄝ彩ㄘㄞ蛋ㄉㄢ

dà lǐ shí wén fù huó jié cǎi dàn

大理石纹复活节彩蛋

Fingerprinted Easter Eggs
手ㄕㄡ畫ㄏㄨㄚ復ㄈㄨ活ㄏㄨㄛ節ㄐㄧㄝ彩ㄘㄞ蛋ㄉㄢ

shǒu huà fù huó jié cǎi dàn

手画复活节彩蛋

Splatter Painted Easter Eggs
噴濺復活節彩蛋
pēn jiàn fù huó jié cǎi dàn
喷溅复活节彩蛋

Rubber Band Easter Eggs
橡皮筋復活節彩蛋
xiàng pí jīn fù huó jié cǎi dàn
橡皮筋复活节彩蛋

Stone Easter Easter Eggs
石紋復活節彩蛋
shí wén fù huó jié cǎi dàn
石纹复活节彩蛋

Natural Dyes for Easter Eggs
自然復活節彩蛋
zì rán rǎn sè fù huó jié cǎi dàn
自然染色复活节彩蛋

Floral Easter Eggs
花朵復活節彩蛋
huā duǒ fù huó jié cǎi dàn
花朵复活节彩蛋

給小朋友
兔子蛋工作室

復活節彩蛋染色：

材料：六個雞蛋、六個碗、湯匙、水、鹽、醋、食物染料、軟衛生紙、和舊報紙

也可準備的材料：貼紙、蠟筆、橡皮筋、舊牙刷

煮硬蛋和染色的方法：

1) 把蛋放在鍋底。（不要把蛋重疊。最好分批煮蛋，不要把鍋盛滿。）

2) 把水放進鍋中，漫過雞蛋約一寸。

3) 用大火把水煮開。

4) 煮三分鐘。熄火或把鍋移開爐子。讓蛋留在水中，待涼（約12分鐘）。

5) 把蛋從鍋中取出，放在冷水中，等你能用手拿蛋不會燙手時取出。

6) 把蛋放在攤在桌上的舊報紙上。

7) 把不同的食物染料、水、和醋放進不同的碗裏。

8) 把貼紙貼在蛋上，或用蠟筆在蛋殼上畫圖案。

9) 把蛋放進有顏料水的小碗中。讓蛋浸泡約五分鐘。用湯匙把蛋取出。

10) 用衛生紙把蛋擦乾。

11) 雞蛋染好了！

請看上面其他不同的復活節彩蛋染色方法。

给小朋友
兔子蛋工作室

复活节彩蛋染色：

材料：六个鸡蛋、六个碗、汤匙、水、盐、醋、食物染料、软卫生纸、和旧报纸

也可准备的材料：贴纸、蜡笔、橡皮筋、旧牙刷

煮硬蛋和染色的方法：

1) 把蛋放在锅底。（不要把蛋重叠。最好分批煮蛋，不要把锅盛满。）
2) 把水放进锅中，漫过鸡蛋约一寸。
3) 用大火把水煮开。
4) 煮三分钟。熄火或把锅移开炉子。让蛋留在水中，待凉。（约12分钟）
5) 把蛋从锅中取出，放在冷水中，等你能用手拿蛋不会烫手时取出，
6) 把蛋放在摊在桌上的旧报纸上。
7) 把不同的食物染料、水、和醋放进不同的碗里。
8) 把贴纸贴在蛋上，或用蜡笔在蛋壳上画图案。
9) 把蛋放进有颜料水的小碗中。让蛋浸泡约五分钟。用汤匙把蛋取出。
10) 用卫生纸把蛋擦乾。
11) 鸡蛋染好了！

请看上面其他不同的复活节彩蛋染色方法。

Other activities:

1. Draw many Easter eggs of different colors.
2. Have your family cut large Easter Eggs from colored construction paper. Decorate the large eggs with buttons, yarn, crayon, feathers, or confetti.
3. Go to an egg-hunting party. Enjoy. Tell your family what you do at the party.
4. What do you usually do on Easter? Draw a picture of Easter Fun.
5. What does Easter mean to you?
6. Find out what rabbits eat. Tell your parents or grandparents what rabbits' food is and how you should feed them.

其他活動：

1. 畫許多不同顏色的復活節彩蛋。
2. 和你的家人把彩色勞作紙剪成許多大大的復活節彩蛋。用鈕子、毛線、蠟筆、羽毛、或彩色碎紙裝飾這些大彩蛋。
3. 參加一個找彩蛋的派對。希望你玩得開心。然後告訴你的家人你們在派對做了什麼。
4. 你平常復活節做什麼？畫一張好玩兒的復活節圖畫。
5. 你認為復活節是什麼意思？
6. 問一問，查一查，兔子吃什麼。告訴你的父母或祖父母，兔子吃的食物，你會怎麼樣餵兔子。

其他活动：

1. 画许多不同颜色的复活节彩蛋。
2. 和你的家人把彩色劳作纸剪成许多大大的复活节彩蛋。用扣子、毛线、蜡笔、羽毛、或彩色碎纸装饰这些大彩蛋。
3. 参加一个找彩蛋的派对。希望你玩得开心。然後告诉你的家人你们在派对做了什么。
4. 你平常复活节做什么？画一张好玩儿的复活节图画。
5. 你认为复活节是什么意思？
6. 问一问，查一查，兔子吃什么。告诉你的父母或祖父母，兔子吃的食物，你会怎么样喂兔子。

Spider the Web Site

蜘(ㄓ)蛛(ㄓㄨ)網(ㄨㄤˇ)址(ㄓˇ)

zhī zhū wǎng zhǐ
蜘蛛网址

Mildred Shaw & Dr. Loretta Huang 杜(dù)英(yīng)慈(cí)

Illustrated by Milo Elea Xu

Spider the Web Site

蜘蛛網址
zhī zhū wǎng zhǐ
蜘蛛网址

I'm just a spider, really tiny,
My web is often bright and shiny.
I watch you as you come and go
Right by your clear kitchen window.
I am not big, black and hairy
So I can't be very scary.

My web is dainty yet so strong
It catches insects all day long.
My web's my home, I'm often there
Watching insects caught in my snare.
I eat bugs, mosquitoes and gnats
On my menu, they make good snacks.
What I have learned to enjoy so much
Are mosquitoes with the West-Nile touch.
These insects I eat more and more
Their flavor I really adore.
When out walking, my web you spy
Please don't disturb it, walk on by.
I can always spin and repair
But be cautious if I am there.

Killing insects with deadly diseases
Is always something that truly pleases.
Mosquitoes with virus of the West Nile
I exterminate, and I make you smile.
So keep me healthy and give me space !
I am important in nature's place !

Words of wisdom:

When spide webs unite, they can tie up a lion.
(Ethiopian Proverb)

智慧之語：蜘蛛網合起來可以綁住一頭獅子（伊索比亞諺語）

zhì huì zhī yǔ zhī zhū wǎng hé qǐ lái kě yǐ bǎng zhù yī tóu shī zǐ
智慧之语：蜘蛛网合起来可以绑住一头狮子
yī suǒ bǐ yà yàn yǔ
（伊索比亚谚语）

Spider the Web Site

I'm just a spider, really tiny,
My web is often bright and shiny.

蜘ㄓㄨ 蛛ㄓㄨ 網ㄨㄤˇ 址ㄓˇ

我ㄨㄛˇ只ㄓˇ是ㄕˋ一一隻ㄓ蜘ㄓ蛛ㄓㄨ，真ㄓㄣ的ㄉㄜ˙非ㄈㄟ常ㄔㄤˊ小ㄒㄧㄠˇ，
我ㄨㄛˇ的ㄉㄜ˙網ㄨㄤˇ子ㄗ˙常ㄔㄤˊ常ㄔㄤˊ又ㄧㄡˋ明ㄇㄧㄥˊ亮ㄌㄧㄤˋ又ㄧㄡˋ閃ㄕㄢˇ耀ㄧㄠˋ。

zhī zhū wǎng zhǐ
蜘蛛网址

wǒ zhǐ shì yī zhǐ zhī zhū zhēn dì fēi cháng xiǎo
我只是一只蜘蛛，真的非常小，
wǒ dì wǎng zǐ cháng cháng shì yòu míng liàng yòu shǎn yào
我的网子常常是又明亮又闪耀。

Spider the Web Site

I watch you as you come and go
Right by your clear kitchen window.

我ㄨㄛˇ看ㄎㄢˋ你ㄋㄧˇ去ㄑㄩˋ去ㄑㄩˋ來ㄌㄞˊ來ㄌㄞˊ

經ㄐㄧㄥ過ㄍㄨㄛˋ你ㄋㄧˇ乾ㄍㄢ淨ㄐㄧㄥˋ的ㄉㄜ˙廚ㄔㄨˊ房ㄈㄤˊ窗ㄔㄨㄤ台ㄊㄞˊ。

wǒ kàn nǐ qù qù lái lái
我 看 你 去 去 来 来

jīng guò nǐ qián jìng dì chú fáng chuāng tái
经过你乾净的厨房窗台。

I am not big, black and hairy
So I can't be very scary.

我不是又大又黑又有毛
所以我不可能是很可怕讓你心裏發毛。

wǒ bù shì yòu dà yòu hēi yòu yǒu máo
我不是又大又黑又有毛
suǒ yǐ wǒ bù kě néng shì hěn kě pà ràng nǐ xīn lǐ fā máo
所以我不可能是很可怕让你心里发毛。

Spider the Web Site

My web is dainty yet so strong
It catches insects all day long.

我的網子雖然小巧但是很堅牢
它整天捉蟲子真不少。

wǒ dí wǎng zǐ suī rán xiǎo qiǎo dàn shì hěn jiān láo
我的网子虽然小巧但是很坚牢
tā zhěng tiān zhuō chóng zǐ zhēn bù shǎo
它整天捉虫子真不少。

Spider the Web Site

My web's my home, I'm often there;
Watching insects caught in my snare.

我的網子就是我的家，
我常常都在那裏；
看著蟲子被捉進我的羅網裏。

wǒ di wǎng zǐ jiù shì wǒ di jiā　wǒ cháng cháng dū zài nà lǐ
我的网子就是我的家，我常常都在那里；
kàn zhuó chóng zǐ bèi zhuō jìn wǒ di luó wǎng lǐ
看着虫子被捉进我的罗网里。

I eat bugs, mosquitoes and gnats
On my menu, they make good snacks.

我吃昆蟲、蚊子、和蚋蟲
在我的菜單上，他們都是好點心。

wǒ chī kūn chóng　wén zǐ　hé ruì chóng
我吃昆虫、蚊子、和蚋虫
zài wǒ dì cài dān shàng　tā men dū shì hǎo diǎn xīn
在我的菜单上，他们都是好点心。

What I have learned to enjoy so much
Are mosquitoes with the
West-Nile touch.

我已經學會吃最喜歡的食物
那就是蚊子帶著西尼羅河病毒。

我已经学会吃最喜欢的食物
wǒ yǐ jīng xué huì chī zuì xǐ huān di shí wù

那就是蚊子带着西尼罗河病毒。
nà jiù shì wén zǐ dài zhuó xī ní luó hé bìng dú

These insects I eat more and more
Their flavor I really adore.

這些蟲子我愈吃愈多
它們的美味我真正愛上了。

zhè xiē chóng zǐ wǒ yù chī yù duō
这些虫子我愈吃愈多

tā men dì měi wèi wǒ zhēn zhèng ài shàng liǎo
它们的美味我真正爱上了。

Spider the Web Site

When out walking, my web you spy
Please don't disturb it, walk on by.

當ㄉㄤ你ㄋㄧˇ外ㄨㄞˋ出ㄔㄨ散ㄙㄢˋ步ㄅㄨˋ看ㄎㄢˋ見ㄐㄧㄢˋ我ㄨㄛˇ的ㄉㄜ˙網ㄨㄤˇ

請ㄑㄧㄥˇ不ㄅㄨˋ要ㄧㄠˋ打ㄉㄚˇ擾ㄖㄠˇ它ㄊㄚ，要ㄧㄠˋ繼ㄐㄧˋ續ㄒㄩˋ走ㄗㄡˇ過ㄍㄨㄛˋ蜘ㄓ蛛ㄓㄨ網ㄨㄤˇ。

dāng　nǐ　wài　chū　sàn　bù　kàn　jiàn　wǒ　dī　wǎng
当你外出散步看见我的网

qǐng　bù　yào　dǎ　rǎo　tā　　　yào　jì　xù　zǒu　guò　zhī　zhū　wǎng
请不要打扰它，要继续走过蜘蛛网。

I can always spin and repair
But be cautious if I am there.

我ㄨㄛˇ會ㄏㄨㄟˋ一ㄧ直ㄓˊ結ㄐㄧㄝˊ網ㄨㄤˇ和ㄏㄜˊ修ㄒㄧㄡ補ㄅㄨˇ蜘ㄓ蛛ㄓㄨ網ㄨㄤˇ

但ㄉㄢˋ是ㄕˋ請ㄑㄧㄥˇ特ㄊㄜˋ別ㄅㄧㄝˊ小ㄒㄧㄠˇ心ㄒㄧㄣ， 如ㄖㄨˊ果ㄍㄨㄛˇ我ㄨㄛˇ在ㄗㄞˋ網ㄨㄤˇ上ㄕㄤˋ。

wǒ huì yī zhí jié wǎng hé xiū bǔ zhī zhū wǎng
我会一直结网和修补蜘蛛网

dàn shì qǐng tè bié xiǎo xīn　 rú guǒ wǒ zài wǎng shàng
但是请特别小心，如果我在网上。

Killing insects with deadly diseases
Is always something that truly pleases.

殺死帶致命病毒的蟲子
總是真正開心的事。

shā sǐ dài zhì mìng bìng dú dì chóng zǐ
杀死带致命病毒的虫子
zǒng shì zhēn zhèng kāi xīn dì shì
总是真正开心的事。

Mosquitoes with virus of the West Nile
I exterminate, and I make you smile.

帶著西尼羅河病毒的蚊子
我捕滅了它，會讓你微笑歡喜。

dài zhuó xī ní luó hé bìng dú dì wén zǐ
带着西尼罗河病毒的蚊子
wǒ pū miè liǎo tā　huì ràng nǐ wēi xiào huān xǐ
我扑灭了它，会让你微笑欢喜。

So keep me healthy and give me space !
I am important in nature's place !

所以請保護我的健康和賜給我空間！
我在自然界的地位是很重要的！

suǒ yǐ qǐng bǎo hù wǒ dī jiàn kāng hé cì gěi wǒ kōng jiān
所以请保护我的健康和赐给我空间！
wǒ zài zì rán jiè dī dī wèi shì hěn zhòng yào dī
我在自然界的地位是很重要的！

Interesting Facts about Spiders for Children

1. Spiders are *air breathing* and have eight legs.
2. Spiders live everywhere in the world except for *Antarctica*.
3. As of August 2022, *scientists (taxonomists)* have recorded more than 50,356 spider *species* and 132 families.
4. Spider webs *vary* widely in size, shape, and the amount of sticky thread used.
5. Spiders have been found in rocks from 318-299 *million* years ago.
6. A *vegetarian* species was *described* in 2008, but all other known species prey on insects and other spiders. A few large *species* also take birds and lizards.
7. Spiders have jaws and teeth but cannot chew Spiders' *intestines* are too narrow to take *solids*, and they *liquidize* their food by flooding it with *digestive* enzymes, and grinding it with the bases of their *appendages* ahead of the mouth.
8. *Female* spiders weave silk egg *sacs*, each of which may *contain* hundreds of eggs.
9. *Females* of many *species* care for their young. They may carry the babies around or by sharing food with them.
10. A *minority* of species are social, building *communal* webs that may house anywhere from a few to 50,000 *individuals*.
11. *Male* spiders *identify* themselves by a variety of complex *courtship rituals* to avoid being eaten by the females. Males of most species *survive* a few matings, limited by their short life spans.
12. Most spiders live for at most two years.
13. Some large *species* of spiders such as tarantula can live up to 25 years in *captivity*.
14. A few *species* of spiders have *venom* that is *dangerous* to humans.
15. *Scientists* are now *researching* the use of spider *venom* in *medicine* and as non-polluting pesticides.
16. Spider silk provides a *combination of lightness, strength* and *elasticity* that is *superior* to that of *synthetic materials*.
17. Most spiders have four pairs of eyes (8) on the top-front area of the head.

18. *Bristles* on spiders are touch *sensors*, *responding* to different levels of force, from strong *contact* to very weak air *currents*.
19. *Chemical sensors* provide tastes and smell.
20. Spiders have in the joints of their *limbs*, device that *detects* forces and *vibrations*.
21. The spider's *abdomen* has one to four (usually three) pairs of movable *spinnerets* which *emit silk*.
22. Silk is mainly *composed* of a *protein*. They may use silk to catch *prey*, or wrap around *fertilized* eggs, as a safety rope for nest building, or as *parachutes* by the young of some species.
23. Females lay up to 3,000 eggs in one or more silk egg sacs.
24. In some *species, females* die afterwards, but females of other species protect the sacs by *attaching* them to their webs, hiding them in nests, carrying them or *dragging* them along.
25. Baby spiders pass all their *larval stages* inside the egg and hatch as *spiderlings*.
26. Some spiders care for their young by carrying the *brood* on the *rough bristles* on the mother's back.
27. Spiders have to *molt* (*remove* their skins) as their skins cannot stretch.
28. Spiders occur in a large range of sizes. The smallest are tiny in body length. The largest and heaviest spider *tarantulas* can have body lengths up to 3.5 inches (90 mm) and leg span up to 10 inches (250 mm).
29. Most spiders will only bite in *self-defense*, and few produce worse *effects* than a mosquito bite or bee sting.
30. *Funnel web spiders, Brazilian wandering spider, recluse* and *widow spiders* are *aggressive* and their *venom* has *resulted* in human deaths.
31. Cooked *tarantula* spiders are *considered a delicacy* in Cambodia and by the Piaroa Indians of southern Venezuela.
32. Spider *venoms* may be a less *polluting alternative* to *conventional pesticides* as they are deadly to insects but the great *majority* is harmless to *vertebrates*. The Australian *funnel* web spiders are a promising source.

* Only *female* mosquitos bite, and they use the *protein* in our blood to *develop* the eggs. Mosquitos can hatch and develop into adults in seven days.
* *Symptoms* of the *West Nile Virus* can *include* fever, headache, body aches, *nausea* or *skin rash*. Severe cases can lead to *paralysis* or even death.

給小朋友
有關蜘蛛的有趣常識

1. 蜘蛛呼吸空氣，它有八條腿。
2. 蜘蛛除了南極之外，住在世界各地。
3. 到 2022 年 8 月，科學家（昆蟲學家）鑑定了 50,356 個品種和 132 個族類的蜘蛛。
4. 蜘蛛網的大小形狀和吐粘絲的分量大有不同。
5. 蜘蛛被發現在二、三億年前的岩石裏。
6. 在 2008 年，發現有素食的蜘蛛品種。但是其他品種的蜘蛛都吃昆蟲。少數大體型的蜘蛛品種也吃鳥和四腳蛇。
7. 蜘蛛有牙和顎，但是不能嚼。蜘蛛的腸子太窄，不能容納固體食物。它們用大量的消化酶素把食物化成液體，用嘴前面的器官把食物磨碎。
8. 母蜘蛛網織絲質的蛋囊，每個袋子可能有幾百個蛋。
9. 很多品種的母蜘蛛照顧她們的小寶寶。她們也可能會帶著寶寶走動，或是和寶寶們分享食物。
10. 少數的蜘蛛品種是社會蜘蛛，它們建造公社蜘蛛網，有幾隻甚至五萬隻（50,000）蜘蛛住在網上。
11. 公蜘蛛用複雜的求偶儀式來表達他的身份，以免被母蜘蛛吃掉。多數品種的公蜘蛛能交配幾次,但只限于他短暫的生命期限。

12. 大多數的蜘蛛最多活兩年。

13. 有些大蜘蛛,像有毛的毒蜘蛛,被飼養可以活25年。

14. 少數蜘蛛品種有危害人類的毒液。

15. 科學家現在正在研究用蜘蛛的毒液在醫藥用途上和不會污染環境的殺蟲劑。

16. 蜘蛛絲體輕、強韌、有彈性,比合成材料優良多了。

17. 多數的蜘蛛有四對(8個)眼睛,長在頭頂前部。

18. 蜘蛛身上的毛刺是它的觸覺器官,可以覺察到不同程度的力量,從很強的衝擊到很弱的氣流都能感覺到。

19. 它的化學感應器主控味覺和嗅覺。

20. 蜘蛛腳的關節有器官察覺力量和震動。

21. 蜘蛛腹部有一對到四對(通常三對)可以吐絲的吐絲器。

22. 蜘蛛絲主要是由蛋白質組成的。它們用絲捕捉獵物,或包裹受精卵,或是造窩時的安全繩子,或是某些品種的小寶寶的降落傘。

23. 母蜘蛛可以在一個或好幾個蛋囊中生到三千個(3,000)蛋。

24. 有些品種的母蜘蛛生完蛋就死了。但是其他品种的母蜘蛛保護蛋囊,把它黏在蜘蛛網上,或是藏起來,帶著走,或拖著蛋囊走。

25. 蜘蛛寶寶們在蛋中孵化， 小蜘蛛最後破蛋而出。

26. 有些蜘蛛照顧寶寶， 把小蜘蛛們帶在媽媽背上的粗毛上。

27. 蜘蛛必須要脫皮長大， 因為它們的皮膚不能伸展。

28. 蜘蛛的尺寸有很大的差距。 最小的蜘蛛身体只有一丁點兒。 最大最重的有毒毛蜘蛛， 身長有90公分 （3.5英吋）， 連它的腳可有 250 公分 （10英吋）。

29. 大多數的蜘蛛， 只有在自衛的時候才咬人。 只有少數的蜘蛛造成比蚊子咬、 蜜蜂叮更壞的結果。

30. 漏斗網蜘蛛、 巴西遊走蜘蛛、 隱士蜘蛛、 寡婦蜘蛛有攻擊性， 它們的毒液造成人類的死亡。

31. 在 Cambodia 和 Venezuela 南部的印地安人把燒熟的大蜘蛛當成美味的一道菜。

32. 蜘蛛的毒液可能是比較不污染自然環境的另類殺蟲劑， 它對昆蟲有致命的殺傷力， 但是對脊椎動物無害。 澳大利亞的漏斗網蜘蛛是很有前途的來源。

* 只有母蚊蟲才咬人， 它們用我們血中的蛋白質滋養它們的蛋。 蛋在七天之內就孵化成蚊蟲了。

* 西尼羅河病毒的症狀包括： 發燒、 頭疼、 身體痛、 嘔吐、 皮膚發疹子、 嚴重時可以造成癱瘓或死亡。

给小朋友
有关蜘蛛的有趣常识

1. 蜘蛛呼吸空气,它有八条腿。
2. 蜘蛛除了南极之外,住在世界各地。
3. 到2022年8月,科学家(昆虫家)鉴定了50,356个品种和132个族类的蜘蛛。
4. 蜘蛛网的大小形状和吐粘丝的分量大有不同。
5. 蜘蛛被发现在二、三亿年前的岩石里。
6. 在2008年,发现有素食的蜘蛛品种。但是其他品种的蜘蛛都吃昆虫。少数大体型的蜘蛛品种也吃鸟和四脚蛇。
7. 蜘蛛有牙和颚,但是不能嚼。蜘蛛的肠子太窄,不能容纳固体食物。它们用大量的消化酶素把食物化成液体,用嘴前面的器官把食物磨碎。
8. 母蜘蛛网织丝质的蛋囊,每个袋子可能有几百个蛋。
9. 很多品种的母蜘蛛照顾她们的小宝宝。她们也可能会带着宝宝走动,或是和宝宝们分享食物。
10. 少数的蜘蛛品种是社会蜘蛛,它们建造公社蜘蛛网,有几只甚至五万只(50,000)蜘蛛住在网上。
11. 公蜘蛛用复杂的求偶仪式来表达他的身份,以免被母蜘蛛吃掉。多数品种的公蜘蛛能交配几次,但只限于他短暂的生命期限。
12. 大多数的蜘蛛最多活两年。
13. 有些大蜘蛛,像有毛的毒蜘蛛,被饲养可以活25年。
14. 少数蜘蛛品种有危害人类的毒液。

15. 科学家现在正在研究用蜘蛛的毒液在医药用途上和不会污染环境的杀虫剂。
16. 蜘蛛丝体轻、强韧、有弹性，比合成材料优良多了。
17. 多数的蜘蛛有四对（8个）眼睛，长在头顶前部。
18. 蜘蛛身上的毛刺是它的触觉器官，可以觉察到不同程度的力量，从很强的冲击到很弱的气流都能感觉到。
19. 它的化学感应器主控味觉和嗅觉。
20. 蜘蛛脚的关节有器官察觉力量和震动。
21. 蜘蛛腹部有一对到四对（通常三对）可以动的射丝器射出蜘蛛丝。
22. 蜘蛛丝主要是由蛋白质组成。它们用丝捕捉猎物，或包裹受精卵，或是造窝时的安全绳子，或是某些品种的小宝宝的降落伞。
23. 母蜘蛛可以在一个或好几个蛋囊中生到三千个（3,000）蛋。
24. 有些品种的母蜘蛛生完蛋就死了。但是其他品种的母蜘蛛保护蛋囊，把它粘在蜘蛛网上，或是藏起来，带着走，或拖着蛋囊走。
25. 蜘蛛宝宝们在蛋中孵化，小蜘蛛最后破蛋而出。
26. 有些蜘蛛照顾宝宝，把小蜘蛛们带在妈妈背上的粗毛上。
27. 蜘蛛必须要脱皮长大，因为它们的皮肤不能伸展。
28. 蜘蛛的尺寸有很大的差距。最小的蜘蛛身体只有一丁点儿。最大最重的有毒毛蜘蛛，身长有90公分（3.5英寸），连它的脚可有 250 公分（10英寸）。
29. 大多数的蜘蛛，只有在自卫的时候才咬人。只有少数的蜘蛛 造成比蚊子咬、蜜蜂叮更坏的结果。
30. 漏斗网蜘蛛、巴西游走蜘蛛、隐士蜘蛛、寡妇蜘蛛有攻击性，它们的毒液造成人类的死亡。

31. 在 Cambodia 和 Venezuela 南部的印地安人把烧熟的大蜘蛛当成美味的一道菜。

32. 蜘蛛的毒液可能是比较不污染自然环境的另类杀虫剂，它对昆虫有致命杀伤力，但是对脊椎动物无害。澳大利亚的漏斗网蜘蛛是很有前途的来源。

- 只有母蚊虫才咬人，它们用我们血中的蛋白质滋养它们的蛋。蛋在七天之内就孵化成蚊虫了。
- 西尼罗河病毒的症状包括：发烧、头疼、身体痛、呕吐、皮肤发疹子、严重时可以造成瘫痪或死亡。

Spider Workshop for Children

1. Find a spider near your home and answer the following questions with your family or teacher.
   - Where in the world does your spider live?
   - Describe the environment your spider lives in.
   - What does your spider eat?
   - How does your spider find its food?
   - What type of markings does your spider have?
   - How does your spider protect itself?
   - Describe three more interesting things that you have learned about your spider.

2. Write it down if you can.

   _____
   _____
   _____
   _____
   _____
   _____
   _____

3. Search the internet for more information about spiders around the world.

4. Look at the following worksheets and do the arts and crafts with help from your family and teacher.

Name _____

Spiders are *Arachnids*.
They live everywhere in the world.

All spiders have:
- eight legs
- a spinneret that spins silk
- fangs
- jaws and teeth but cannot chew

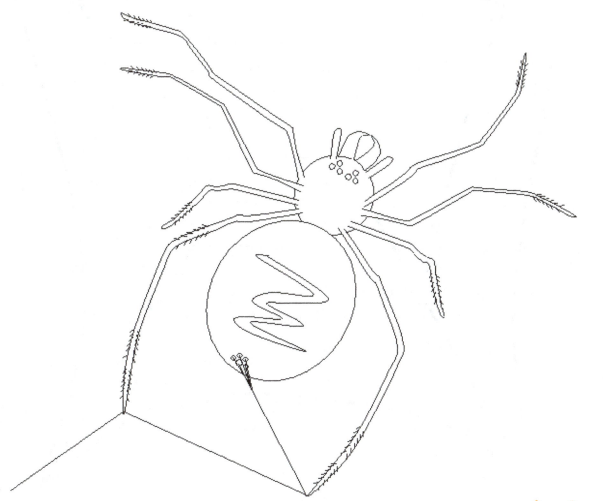

Color the pictures of the spider. Write interesting facts about spiders.

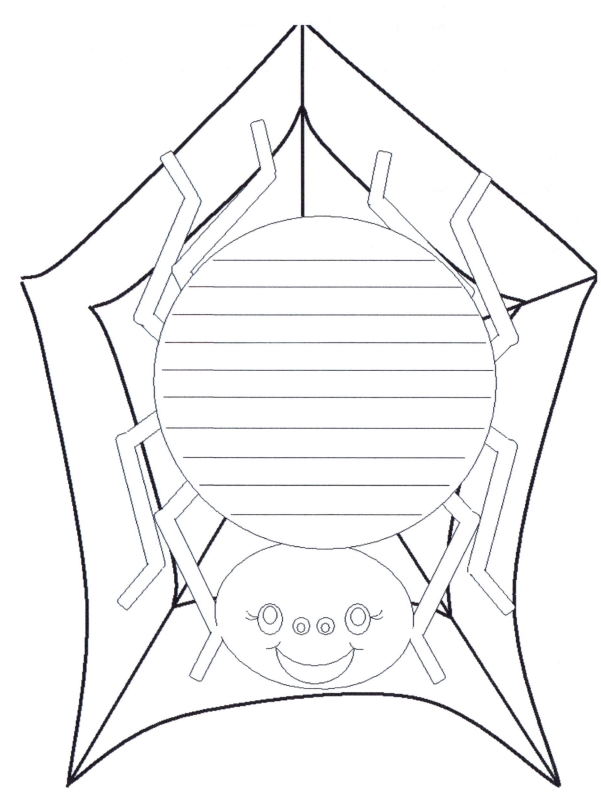

Make the finger puppets for finger play. Color the pieces.
Cut out the pieces. Glue the end of the loop to fit your fingers.
(You may make a copy of the pictures, then color and cut.)

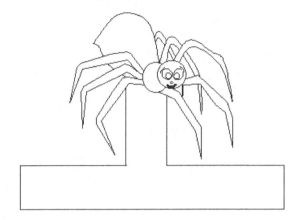

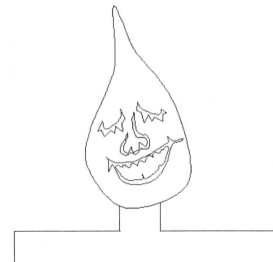

給小朋友
蜘蛛工作室

1. 在你家的附近找一隻蜘蛛。 向家人或老師回答下面的問題。
   - 你的蜘蛛住在世界的什麼地方？
   - 你的蜘蛛住在什麼自然環境裏？
   - 你的蜘蛛吃什麼？
   - 它如何尋找食物？
   - 你的蜘蛛身上有什麼花紋？
   - 你的蜘蛛怎麼樣保護自己？
   - 說一說你還學到三樣有關于蜘蛛有趣的知識。
2. 你能把你學到的寫下了嗎？
3. 在網絡上搜尋有關世界各地蜘蛛的知識。
4. 看看下面的圖，和家人或老師一同做些勞作。

把上面的蜘蛛圖畫塗上顏色：

蜘蛛和蜈蚣、 臭蟲屬于同一類的昆蟲。 它們住在世界各地。 所有的蜘蛛都有八條腿、 可以吐絲的吐絲器、 尖牙、 和不能嚼的牙齒與顎。

勞作：

用小蜘蛛、 太陽、 和水珠的圖片做指頭玩偶。 圖片塗上顏色， 用剪刀剪下，把紙圈兩頭黏起， 適合兒童指頭的大小， 就成了指頭玩偶。
（ 可以先把圖片用影印機印出一張紙，塗色再剪。 ）

给小朋友
蜘蛛工作室

1. 在你家的附近找一只蜘蛛。向家人或老师回答下面的问题。
   * 你的蜘蛛住在世界的什么地方？
   * 你的蜘蛛住在什么自然环境里？
   * 你的蜘蛛吃什么？
   * 它如何寻找食物？
   * 你的蜘蛛身上有什么花纹？
   * 你的蜘蛛怎么样保护自己？
   * 说一说你还学到三样有关于蜘蛛有趣的知识。
2. 你能把你学到的写下了吗？
3. 在网络上搜寻有关世界各地蜘蛛的知识。
4. 看看下面的图，和家人或老师一同做些劳作。

把上面的蜘蛛图画涂上颜色：

蜘蛛和蜈蚣、臭虫属于同一类的昆虫。它们住在世界各地。

所有的蜘蛛都有八条腿、可以吐丝的吐丝器、尖牙、和不能嚼的牙齿与颚。

劳作：

用小蜘蛛、太阳、和水珠的图片，做指头玩偶。图片涂上颜色，用剪刀剪下，把纸圈两头黏起，适合儿童指头的大小，就成了指头玩偶。
（可以先把图片用影印机印出一张纸，涂色再剪。）

The Wishing Goldfish

許願的金魚

xǔ yuàn dí jīn yú
许愿的金鱼

Mildred Shaw & Dr. Loretta Huang 杜英慈 dù yīng cí

Illustrated by Gina Chang 张彦珺 zhāng yàn jùn

The Wishing Fish

In a little glass bowl lived two gold fish,
So bored were they, they began to wish.
Instead of just always swimming around,
They wanted to try walking on the ground.
We're so tired of stale fish food.
Something more tasty would change our mood.
We both wish we had wings so we could fly
Like the buzzing bee that we saw go by.
Or like the robin that can fly and sing.
We wish we could do all of those things.

Suddenly they heard a voice in their bowl.
A mermaid appeared from a magic hole.
"Hello little fish, I've been watching you.
I see why you're bored, with nothing to do."
The gold fish asked her, "What is a mermaid?"
"I'm a sea princess that's come to your aid;
I'm a magic lady with a fish tail
Who can grant many wishes without fail.
I can turn your fins into wings that fly.
That way you can soar high up in the sky.
Breathing fresh dry air now as you come down,
You can live your life freely on the ground?'

Then, the mermaid saw the cute little pair
Come down so happily out of the air.
But the goldfish quite soon did realize
No more could they swim, to their great surprise.
They had fun for awhile, soaring up high,
But they really disliked their skins so dry.
They wished to go back to their swimming ways,
Gliding through the water could brighten their days.
So the mermaid found them a huge fish tank
With other fish friends in the water they sank.

They both know now more that ever before,
It's really the water that they adore!

Words of wisdom:

Be careful what you wish for.

智ㄓˋ慧ㄏㄨㄟˋ小ㄒㄧㄠˇ語ㄩˇ： 小ㄒㄧㄠˇ心ㄒㄧㄣ地ㄉㄧ˙真ㄓㄣ心ㄒㄧㄣ許ㄒㄩˇ願ㄩㄢˋ

zhì　huì　xiǎo　yǔ　　　xiǎo　xīn　dì　zhēn　xīn　xǔ　yuàn

智慧小语：小心地真心许愿

Note: The singular and plural form of "fish" or "goldfish" is the same.

"fish" 及ㄐㄧˊ "goldfish" 單ㄉㄢ數ㄕㄨˋ多ㄉㄨㄛ數ㄕㄨˋ都ㄉㄨ是ㄕˋ同ㄊㄨㄥˊ一ㄧˋ樣ㄧㄤˋ的ㄉㄜ˙英ㄧㄥ文ㄨㄣˊ字ㄗˋ；

"fish" 及 "goldfish" 单数多数都是同一样的英文字。

dān shù duō shù dū shì tóng yī yàng dī yīng wén zì

The Wishing Fish

In a little glass bowl lived two gold fish,
So bored were they, they began to wish.

許願的金魚

在小小的玻璃缸裏住了兩條金魚,
真厭煩住在玻璃缸裏,它們就開始許願。

许愿的金鱼

在小小的玻璃缸里住了两条金鱼,
真厌烦住在玻璃缸里,它们就开始许愿。

The Wishing Goldfish

Instead of just always swimming around,
They wanted to try walking on the ground.

不想只在水裏繞著游泳,
它們要試著在地上走動。

bù xiǎng zhǐ zài shuǐ lǐ rào zhù yóu yǒng
不想只在水里绕著游泳,
tā men yào shì zhù zài dì shàng zǒu dòng
它们要试著在地上走动。

The Wishing Goldfish

We're so tired of stale fish food. Something more tasty would change our mood.

"我們吃膩了不新鮮的魚食。更美味的食物會改變我們的心情。

"我们吃腻了不新鲜的鱼食。
更美味的食物会改变我们的心情。

The Wishing Goldfish

We both wish we had wings so we could fly
Like the buzzing bee that we saw go by.

我們倆希望有翅膀能夠飛
就像我們看到飛過去的嗡嗡蜜蜂。

wǒ men liǎ xī wàng yǒu chì bǎng néng gòu fēi
我们俩希望有翅膀能够飞
jiù xiàng wǒ men kàn dào fēi guò qù dì wēng wēng mì fēng
就像我们看到飞过去的嗡嗡蜜蜂。

Or like the robin that can fly and sing.
We wish we could do all of those things.

或者像會飛翔會唱歌的知更鳥兒
我們希望我們能做這些事兒。"

或者像会飞翔会唱歌的知更鸟儿
我们希望我们能做这些事儿。"

The Wishing Goldfish

Suddenly they heard a voice in their bowl.
A mermaid appeared from a magic hole.

忽然它們聽到魚缸裏有一個聲音。
一條美人魚從一個魔術洞裏出現。

忽然它们听到鱼缸里有一个声音。
一条美人鱼从一个魔术洞里出现。

The Wishing Goldfish

"Hello little fish, I've been watching you.
I see why you're bored, with nothing to do."

"你們好嗎小金魚！我一直在注意你，
我是美人魚。
我看到你們沒事做，的確太沒趣。"

"nǐ men hǎo ma xiǎo jīn yú! wǒ yì zhí zài zhù yì nǐ,
你们好吗小金鱼！我一直在注意你，
wǒ shì měi rén yú
我是美人鱼。
wǒ kàn dào nǐ men méi shì zuò, dí què tài méi qù
我看到你们没事做，的确太没趣。"

The Wishing Goldfish

The gold fish asked her, "What is a mermaid?"
"I'm a sea princess that's come to your aid.

金魚就問她,"美人魚是什麼魚?"
"我是海裏的公主,特地來幫助你。

金鱼就问她,"美人鱼是什么鱼?"
"我是海里的公主,特地来帮助你。

The Wishing Goldfish

I'm a magic lady with a fish tail
Who can grant many wishes without fail.

我是能變魔術有魚尾巴的美女
我從來沒有失敗讓很多願望實現。

wǒ shì néng biàn mó shù yǒu yú wěi bā di měi nǚ
我是能变魔术有鱼尾巴的美女
wǒ cóng lái méi yǒu shī bài ràng hěn duō yuàn wàng shí xiàn
我从来没有失败让很多愿望实现。

I can turn your fins into wings that fly.
That way you can soar high up in the sky.

我能把你們的魚鰭變成能飛的翅膀。
那樣你們就能在天空飛翔。

wǒ néng bǎ nǐ men de yú qí biàn chéng néng fēi de chì bǎng
我能把你们的鱼鳍变成能飞的翅膀。
nà yàng nǐ men jiù néng zài tiān kōng fēi xiáng
那样你们就能在天空飞翔。

Breathing fresh, dry air now as you come down,
You can live your life freely on the ground."

現在當你們飛下來呼吸新鮮乾燥的空氣，
你們可以自由自在生活在陸地。"

现在当你们飞下来，呼吸新鲜乾燥的空气，
你们可以自由自在生活在陆地。"

The Wishing Goldfish

Then, the mermaid saw the cute little pair
Come down so happily out of the air.

那時, 美人魚看著一對可愛的小金魚
那麼快樂地從空中飛下地。

nà shí měi rén yú kàn zhù yī duì kě ài dī xiǎo jīn yú
那时，美人鱼看著一对可爱的小金鱼
nà me kuài lè dī cóng kōng zhōng fēi xià dī
那么快乐地从空中飞下地。

The Wishing Goldfish

But the goldfish quite soon did realize
No more could they swim,
to their great surprise.

可是金魚們很快就發覺
它們不再會游泳， 它們太驚覺。

可是金鱼们很快就发觉
kě shì jīn yú men hěn kuài jiù fā jué
它们不再会游泳，它们太惊觉。
tā men bù zài huì yóu yǒng　tā men tài jīng jué

The Wishing Goldfish

They had fun for awhile, soaring up high,
But they really disliked their skins so dry.

它們在高空飛翔一會兒是很有趣,
但是它們真的不喜歡它們乾燥的魚皮。

它们在高空飞翔一会儿是很有趣,
但是它们真的不喜欢它们乾燥的鱼皮。

The Wishing Goldfish

They wished to go back
to their swimming ways,
Gliding through the water
could brighten their days.

它們希望回到它們原來的游泳方式，
在水中滑游度日多麼自在舒適。

tā men xī wàng huí dào tā men yuán lái di yóu yǒng fāng shì
它们希望回到它们原来的游泳方式，
zài shuǐ zhōng huá yóu dù rì duō me zì zài shū shì
在水中滑游度日多么自在舒适。

The Wishing Goldfish

So the mermaid found them a huge fish tank,
With other fish friends in the water
they sank.

所以， 美人魚給金魚找來了
一個巨大的水族缸，
金魚和其他的魚朋友
一同沉下有水的水族缸。

所以，美人鱼给金鱼找来了一个巨大的水族缸，
金鱼和其他的鱼朋友一同沉下有水的水族缸。

The Wishing Goldfish

They both know now more than ever before,
It's really the water that they adore.

它們現在比以前更知道,
水才是它們真正深愛的地方。

tā men xiàn zài bǐ yǐ qián gēng zhī dào
它们现在比以前更知道,
shuǐ cái shì tā men zhēn zhèng shēn ài dì dì fāng
水才是它们真正深爱的地方。

Interesting Information about Goldfish and Mermaids for Children

Goldfish

1. Gold fish, a type of carp, is a very *popular aquarium* pet and *ornamental* fish.

2. Their *colors* range from red, gold, blue, and orange to bronze, brown, gray, black, silver, and white.

3. *Multicolored* goldfish are *produced* by *selective breeding* from plain-colored goldfish.

4. The *common* goldfish is a very *popular* house pet for children. Goldfish as pets are more *popular* than cats and dogs!

5. Goldfish *require* little care compared with many pets.

6. Goldfish differ widely in color and shape. There are many fancy *varieties* of goldfish. Some *common* ones have such names as *fringetail, comet nymph, calico, popeye, lionhead, veiltail* and *fantail*. They have different colors and may have spots of blue, purple, *lavender*, or white.

7. Some goldfish grow only 2-3 inches (5-8 *centimeters*) long, and others grow to more than one foot (30 *centimeters*) in length.

8. Some goldfish can live to be very old. Golden carp have lived more than 50 years. The goldfish *life span* is about ten years, but some may live to 15 years.

9. A *container* with *straight* sides is better than a curved bowl because it gives more *surface* for the *absorption* of air.

10. The water must be clean. Make weekly 10-15% water changes.

11. Goldfish need a water *filter* to keep the water from becoming *toxic*.

12. The water should be about 65 o - 68 o F (18 o - 19 o C). Keeping a goldfish above 72 o C for long periods of time will result in *oxygen deprivation*, which can cause *nerve* and *heart damage*, and can *seriously hamper* the fish *immune system* making them more *susceptible* to many *diseases*. Extreme *changes* of *temperature* are *harmful* to the fish also.

13. Goldfish should be fed once a day

14. If you over feed the fish, the *leftover* food will *remain* in the tank and *pollute* the water, causing your fish to *catch diseases*. Only feed the fish as much food as they *can completely consume* in two to five minutes.

15. They eat ready-made goldfish *flakes*; they may also eat dried worms, bread *crumbs*, water *flees*, and plants.

16. Goldfish has no eyelids. They need shade and hiding place.

17. Reasons for not putting your pet goldfish in a glass bowl: (1) bowls are too small; only big enough for one or two small fish; (2) they do not get enough *oxygen* for healthy fish life; (3) they get dirty too quickly; (4) they are much too small to get *decorations* into.

18. The *ancestor* of the goldfish is a plain-colored fish of China and Japan. They have been bred in the *Orient* for over a thousand years. The Chinese bred goldfish to *produce* beautiful colors, unusual fins, and body forms.

19. The Japanese helped *create* many of the *strange* kinds seen today.

20. In Europe, goldfish has been bred for a hundred years.

21. Goldfish first bred in the United States in 1878. Today there are many goldfish farms in many parts of the United States.

22. When you first put your new goldfish in their new tank, do not just pour them in. Instead, place the bag inside the tank 10 minutes and let the water *temperature equal out*. Gently and *gradually* mix in the water and *release* the fish carefully.

23. If you ever need to *catch* your fish once they have been living in their tank, do not use your hands. A fish's *scales* can be *damaged* very easily and *disease* can be brought upon quickly. Use a jar or get a fish net that will fit in your *aquarium* from the pet shop. Fish should be out of the water for the shortest time possible; they cannot breathe air and will die very quickly if left out of water.

24. Goldfish placed in lakes and rivers soon lose their *striking appearances* and look like their plain colored ancestors.

Mermaids

A mermaid is a *mythical creature* that lives in the sea. *According to popular belief, mermaids* have bodies that are half *human* and half fish. They attract people by their beauty and singing. They can *perform magic* by their magic cap. *Mermaids* are often found in art, poetry, and movies.

給小朋友
有關金魚及美人魚的有趣常識

金魚

1. 金魚是一種鯉魚，是非常受歡迎的水族寵物和裝飾魚。

2. 它們的顏色從紅色、金色、藍色、和橘色，到古銅色、棕色、灰色、黑色、銀白、和白色。

3. 多彩的金魚是由單色金魚選擇配種而成的。

4. 普通的金魚是孩子們非常喜歡的家庭寵物。養金魚做寵物比養貓養狗還多。

5. 和許多寵物比較，金魚需要很少的照顧。

6. 金魚的顏色和體型有很大的不同。有很多種漂亮的金魚。常見的金魚有花邊尾、流星、仙女、印花布、泡泡眼、獅子頭、面紗尾、和扇子尾。它們有不同的顏色，也會有藍色、紫色、淡紫色、和白色的花點。

7. 有些金魚只長到2-3英吋（5-8公分）有的長到1呎多長（30公分）。

8. 有些金魚能活到很老。金鯉魚活到50年以上。一般金魚的壽命大約10年，但是有些能活到15年。

9. 四邊垂直的水缸比弧形的水缸更好，因為它有更多的面積吸取空氣。

10. 魚缸的水必須清潔。每周換10-15%的水。

11. 金魚需要一個濾水器，使水不會有毒素。

12. 水的溫度應該是華氏65-68度（攝氏18-19度）。如果金魚長時間留在水溫72度以上，會造成失氧，會引起神經和心臟的損害，阻礙金魚的免疫系統，使它們更容易生病。大幅度的溫差對魚也有害。

13. 金魚應該一天餵一次。

14. 如果餵魚太多，剩餘的食物會留在水缸裏，污染清水，造成金魚生病。只需餵魚能在2-5分鐘吃完的份量。

15. 金魚吃現成的小片魚食。它們也可以吃乾的小蟲、麵包屑、水虱子、和水草。

16. 金魚沒有眼皮。它們需要陰暗的躲藏地方。

17. 不要把寵物金魚放在圓玻璃缸裏的原因是：

（1）　圓玻璃缸太小，只能放一兩隻小魚；
（2）　圓玻璃缸不能吸收足夠的氧氣給魚健康的身體；
（3）　圓玻璃缸很快就髒了；
（4）　圓玻璃缸太小，放不進漂亮的水族裝飾品。

18. 金魚的祖先是中國和日本普通顏色的魚。它們1000多年來被飼養配種。中國人將金魚交配，產生美麗的顏色，特別的魚鰭和體型。

19. 日本人也幫忙創造了許多現在看到的奇特的金魚。

20. 在歐洲，金魚被飼養交配了100多年。

21. 金魚在1878年開始在美國被飼養。今天在美國許多地方有金魚養殖場。

22. 當你第一次將金魚放進新魚缸裏的時候，不要把它們立刻放進水裏。要先把裝魚的塑膠袋放進魚缸等10分鐘，讓袋裏的溫度和缸裏的溫度平衡了，再輕輕慢慢小心地把金魚放到魚缸裏。

23. 如果你必須抓住在魚缸裏的金魚，千萬不要用手。金魚的魚鱗很容易受損，魚就容易生病。用一個乾淨的小瓶或小碗 或是寵物店裏買的小魚網。魚盡量少出水；它們不能呼吸空氣，離開水會很快死亡。

24. 把金魚放在湖裏河裏，不久就會失掉它們特殊的樣子，變成像它們普通顏色的祖先。

美人魚

美人魚是住在海中的神話生物。一般人相信，美人魚有半人半魚的身體。她們以美貌和歌聲引人。她們用她她們的魔術帽子使用魔法。在藝術、詩歌、和電影中常見到美人魚。

给小朋友

有关金鱼及美人鱼的有趣常识

金鱼

1. 金鱼是一种鲤鱼，是非常受欢迎的水族宠物和装饰鱼。
2. 它们的颜色从红色、金色、蓝色、和橘色，到古铜色、棕色、灰色、黑色、银白、和白色。
3. 多彩的金鱼是由单色金鱼选择配种而成的。
4. 普通的金鱼是孩子们非常喜欢的家庭宠物。养金鱼做宠物比养猫养狗还多。
5. 和许多宠物比较，金鱼需要很少的照顾。
6. 金鱼的颜色和体型有很大的不同。有很多种漂亮的金鱼。常见的金鱼有花边尾、流星、仙女、印花布、泡泡眼、狮子头、面纱尾、和扇子尾。它们有不同的颜色，也会有蓝色、紫色、淡紫色、和白色的花点。
7. 有些金鱼只长到 2-3 英寸（5-8 公分）有的长到 1 尺多长（30 公分）。
8. 有些金鱼能活到很老。金鲤鱼活到 50 年以上。一般金鱼的寿命大约 10 年，但是有些能活到 15 年。
9. 四边垂直的水缸比弧形的水缸更好，因为它有更多的面积吸取空气。
10. 鱼缸的水必须清洁。每周换 10-15% 的水。
11. 金鱼需要一个滤水器，使水不会有毒素。
12. 水的温度应该是华氏 65-68 度（摄氏 18-19 度）。如果金鱼长时间留在水温 72 度以上，会造成失氧，会引起神经和心脏的损害，阻碍金鱼的免疫系统，使它们更容易生病。大幅度的温差对鱼也有害。
13. 金鱼应该一天喂一次。

14. 如果喂鱼太多，剩余的食物会留在水缸里，污染清水，造成金鱼生病。只需喂鱼能在2-5分钟吃完的份量。

15. 金鱼吃现成的小片鱼食。它们也可以吃乾的小虫、面包屑、水虱子、和水草。

16. 金鱼没有眼皮。它们需要阴暗的躲藏地方。

17. 不要把宠物金鱼放在圆玻璃缸里的原因是：（1）圆玻璃缸太小，只能放一两只小鱼；（2）圆玻璃缸不能吸收足够的氧气给鱼健康的身体；（3）圆玻璃缸很快就脏了；（4）圆玻璃缸太小，放不进漂亮的水族装饰品。

18. 金鱼的祖先是中国和日本普通颜色的鱼。它们1000多年来被饲养配种。中国人将金鱼交配，产生美丽的颜色，特别的鱼鳍和体型。

19. 日本人也帮忙创造了许多现在看到的奇特的金鱼。

20. 在欧洲，金鱼被饲养交配了100多年。

21. 金鱼在1878年开始在美国被饲养。今天在美国许多地方有金鱼养殖场。

22. 当你第一次将金鱼放进新鱼缸里的时候，不要把它们立刻放进水里要先把装鱼的塑胶袋放进鱼缸等10分钟，让袋里的温度和缸里的温度平衡了，再轻轻慢慢小心地把金鱼放到鱼缸里。

23. 如果你必须抓住在鱼缸里的金鱼，千万不要用手。金鱼的鱼鳞很容易受损，鱼就容易生病。用一个乾净的小瓶或小碗 或是宠物店里买的小鱼网。鱼尽量少出水；它们不能呼吸空气，离开水会很快死亡。

24. 把金鱼放在湖里河里，不久就会失掉它们特殊的样子，变成像它们普通颜色的祖先。

美人鱼

美人鱼是住在海中的神话生物。一般人相信，美人鱼有半人半鱼的身体。她们以美貌和歌声引人。她们用她她们的魔术帽子使用魔法。在艺术、诗歌、

hé diàn yǐng zhōng cháng jiàn dào měi rén yú
和电影中常见到美人鱼。

Goldfish and Mermaid Workshop

1. With your family, visit a pet store, a pet supplies store, or the pet section of Wal-Mart store to observe goldfish in the aquarium tanks. Tell your family or friends what you see. Can you draw some gold fish, in colors, which you have seen?
2. Draw a fish step-by-step.

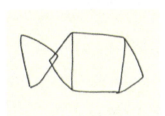

First, draw a square with a pencil.
- Add a *triangle* front and back.
- Add a tilted *triangle tail*.

- Draw the fins.
- Add an eye.
- Draw the mouth, a love heart shape on its side.

- Draw wavy up-and-down stripes.

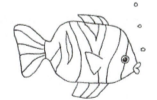

- Erase parts of your squares and triangles to make the body parts join up as in this picture. Round off the tail and body corners.

Here is the fish with a touch of color.

3. Use the computer to search "goldfish types" and see the various types of beautiful gold fish. Would you like to draw some gold fish and keep it in your scrapbooks?

4. Visit a library and find books on gold fish and mermaids. Have your family read the books to you. Can you relate the stories back to your family?

5. Have you ever watched a movie about mermaids or fish? What is the title of the movie? What are the names of the main characters? What does the story tell you?

6. What kinds of pet do you keep at home? Would you like to start a goldfish tank? What do you need to do with your family to prepare an aquarium for your pet goldfish?

Get online and find out how to set up a fish tank for kids. There are many responsibilities, and your parents will need to help you.

金魚和美人魚的工作室

1. 和你的家人去一個寵物店、一個寵物用品店、或是沃瑪商店的寵物部去看看水族箱裏的金魚。告訴你的家人和朋友你看到了什麼樣的金魚。你能用彩色畫些你看到的金魚嗎？

2. 一步一步地畫一條魚。
   - 先用鉛筆畫一個正方形。
   - 在正方形的前面和後面畫兩個三角形。
   - 再加一個斜的三角形尾巴。
   - 畫上魚鰭。
   - 加上一個眼睛。
   - 在邊上畫一個小愛心做它的嘴巴。
   - 畫從上到下彎彎的的條紋。

- 把一部分正方形和三角形的線條用橡皮擦子擦掉，把魚的身體連起來。
- 把魚的尾巴和身體的尖角畫圓。
- 加上幾個小水泡。
- 塗上顏色就成了。

3. 請用電腦搜尋"金魚的種類"，看看不同種的美麗金魚。你要不要畫一些美麗的金魚，放在你的收集簿裏？

4. 去圖書館找一些有關金魚和美人魚的書。請你的家人把書讀給你聽。你能不能把書的內容也講給家人聽呢？

5. 你看過有關美人魚或是魚類的電影嗎？電影的名稱是什麽？主角的名字是什麽？你會講那個故事嗎？

6. 你在家裏養寵物嗎？你想要一個金魚缸嗎？你和家人要怎樣準備一個金魚缸養金魚？請用電腦上網查一查如何給小孩兒準備一個水族箱。養金魚有很多的責任，你的父母必須幫助你。

金鱼和美人鱼的工作室

1. 和你的家人去一个宠物店、一个宠物用品店、或是沃玛商店的宠物部去看看水族箱里的金鱼。告诉你的家人和朋友你看到了什麽样的金鱼。你能用彩色画些你看到的金鱼吗？

2. 一步一步地画一条鱼。
   - 先用铅笔画一个正方形。

- 在正方形的前面和后面画两个三角形。
- 再加一个斜的三角形尾巴。
- 画上鱼鳍。
- 加上一个眼睛。
- 在边上画一个小爱心做它的嘴巴。
- 画从上到下弯弯的的条纹。
- 把一部分正方形和三角形的线条用橡皮擦子擦掉，把鱼的身体连起来。
- 把鱼的尾巴和身体的尖角画圆。
- 加上几个小水泡。
- 涂上颜色就成了。

3. 请用电脑搜寻"金鱼的种类"，看看不同种的美丽金鱼。你要不要画一些美丽的金鱼，放在你的收集簿里？

4. 去图书馆找一些有关金鱼和美人鱼的书。请你的家人把书读给你听。你能不能把书的内容也讲给家人听呢？

5. 你看过有关美人鱼或是鱼类的电影吗？电影的名称是什麽？主角的名字是什么？你会讲那个故事吗？

6. 你在家里养宠物吗？你想要一个金鱼缸吗？你和家人要怎样准备一个金鱼缸养金鱼？请用电脑上网查一查如何给小孩儿准备一个水族箱。养金鱼有很多的责任，你的父母必须帮助你。

Authors:

Loretta Huang, Ph.D. (1942--) is a volunteer Director of Museum Operations at International Art Museum of America in San Francisco and the President of the nonprofit East West Eclectic Society. She has an M.A. in Educational Administration, an M.A. and Doctoral degrees in Teaching English as a Second Language (TESL). She taught English to learners of elementary, secondary, adult schools, universities, and graduate school for 60 years. Her lifelong passions are community services and teaching English to multi-cultural students of all ages. She published an autobiography with Amazon in 2020, <u>A Diamond Necklace, an Immigrant's Story.</u>

作者

杜英慈博士（1942--）是舊金山美國國際藝術館的義工營運長，也是非贏利東西精華學會的會長。她擁有教育行政碩士，英語教學碩士及哲學博士。她獻身英語教學從小學、中學、成人教育、大學及研究所共六十年。她畢生的熱愛是服務社區和教導多元文化和各個年齡的人士學習英文。她在 2020 年，由 Amazon 出版了英文自傳【鑽石項鍊，一個移民者的故事】。

杜英慈博士（1942--）是旧金山美国国际艺术馆的义工营运长，也是非营利东西精华学会的会长。她拥有教育行政硕士，英语教学硕士及哲学博士。她献身英语教学从小学、中学、成人教育、大学及研究所共六十年。她毕生的热爱是服务社区和教导多元文化和各个年龄的人士学习英语。她在 2020 年，由 Amazon 出版了英文自传【钻石项链，一个移民者的故事】。

Mildred S. Shaw (1917-2020 age103) was an elementary reading teacher and Resource Specialist in Duarte School District, California. She wrote some unpublished children's poems on animals before and while she was blind for 20 plus years. Dr. Loretta Huang has edited, translated a few of her rhymes, and added "Interesting Facts about the Animals" with "Workshops for Children" to enrich children's learning experiences.

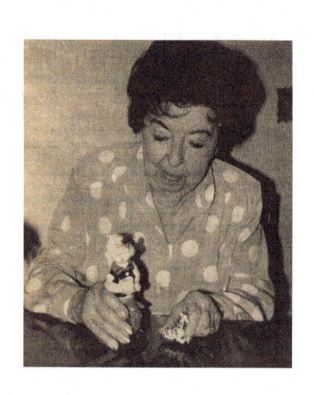

Mildred S. Shaw（1917-2020，享壽103歲）是美國加州杜瓦帝學區的小學閱讀教師和資源專家。她在以前和瞎眼的20多年中，寫了一些沒有出版有關動物的兒童詩。杜英慈博士修改翻譯了幾首，再加上"有關動物的有趣知識"和"兒童工作室"以豐富兒童的學習經驗。

Mildred S. Shaw (1917-2020，享寿103岁）是美国加州杜瓦帝学区的小学阅读教师和资源专家。她在以前和瞎眼的20多年中，写了一些没有出版有关动物的儿童诗。杜英慈博士修改翻译了几首，再加上"有关动物的有趣知识"和"儿童工作室"以丰富儿童的学习经验。

Illustrators:

To encourage talented young people to exert their artistic creativity, all illustrators of the series have been teenagers and young adults in their twenties. Drawings come in various artistic styles----realistic, sketching, and even electronic art, to inspire children's interest.

繪圖者

為了鼓勵年輕人發揮他們的藝術才華，本書的繪圖者都是十多歲和二十多歲的青少年。繪畫的風格有寫實、速寫、和電腦製圖，希望啟發兒童們的興趣。

绘图者

为了鼓励年轻人发挥他们的艺术才华，本书集的绘图者都是十多岁和二十多岁的青少年。绘画的风格有写实、速写、和电脑制图，希望启发儿童们的兴趣。

I especially want to thank Guo Yun and Sophia Lai of China, and Eisen Adorador of the Philippines for helping me put this bilingual Children's book together. It is indeed A LABOR OF LOVE !

我特別要感謝中國的**郭雲、来蕊**和菲律賓的 **Eisen Adorador** 三位年輕女士幫助完成書的排版，使這本雙語童書問世。這真是一本愛的產物！

我特别要感谢中国的**郭云、来蕊**和菲律宾的 **Eisen Adorado** 三位年轻女士帮助完成书的排版，使这本双语童书问世。这真是一本爱的产物！